A Prisoner by No Crime of My Own

From Innocence to Horror
The True Crime Story of
A Child Witness

Jodie Tedder

Brit Diaz

IOI, Inc.

A PRISONER BY NO CRIME
OF MY OWN

Contents

Ode to the Unknown Woman
We met only once but I never forgot you.
You stayed with me in my dreams.
You prodded me on when I wanted to stop.
You were so beautiful and kind.
You saw me. Thank you for that.
Your story lives on with me.
This labor of love, my last gift I give to thee.

To my Girls ~ I wouldn't have made it without you.

To my Grandchildren ~ Generational curses are behind you.

To all Survivors of Childhood Crimes & Families of Missing Persons ~

I stand with you.

Introduction

For our struggle is not against flesh and blood, but against the rulers, against the authorities, against the powers of this dark world and against the spiritual forces of evil in the heavenly realms.

Ephesians 6:12

When I was three and a half years old, I murdered a woman.

I spent the next fifty years retracing and recovering bent memories that had long been buried by the great force of denial. I went back and fought to uncover the truth that had been buried on forty acres, in a sink hole, on my parents' property.

Returning because I too was a murderer. Although only three, I was old enough to feel the guilt when we walked out of that room alive, and she did not. Old enough to know that I shared a secret with my father and his friend that no one else would ever know. We three would stay connected for the rest of our lives, incarcerated together with only each other as accomplices. Not a matter of speaking, but a matter of fact: I am guilty of murder just as they are.

Needing to reconstruct my past, the closer I got to it, the more the pain became real. By getting serious about exploring where I came from, I would not only be called a liar, but also be rejected by the only family I grew up with. The closer to the truth, the deeper the cavern became between me and everything I had ever loved.

With each step I took toward my story, no love would wait for me. No mother to meet me at the end to comfort or soothe. No father to lay me down with a soft blanket at the end of a long day and tell me to rest because I'd done a good job.

If I didn't honor myself by returning to my past, and bringing vindication where possible, I would have been left abandoned. Not by them, I would have abandoned myself. I had to force myself to remember me. Everything told me to stop seeking, stop turning over rocks. "Learn to live," they would tell me. Didn't they see that's exactly what I was doing? My goals to uncover my past made other people extremely uncomfortable. No one liked hearing my story. Not just my family, but friends, acquaintances, and all the rest who happened along during the years. Uncovering my past was a way out of the forest of abandonment. Trees of denial and thickets of shame kept me hidden in darkness.

At many times I felt as if going in reverse. Always waiting for the trip that would take me to the promised land, and then finding it was just another place to explore. Yet, I kept my feet propelling forward on this road. It took me forty years to find my entire story and uncover who I really am, with daily life occurring around the process of growing up. It preoccupied my days, stole my nights, and it intertwined with every relationship I had.

The way out of pain is not the course I imagined -- a few counseling sessions, speaking and acting with forgiveness, spending some time to grieve, and be done. Not true. It takes a journey that only the brave survives. My faith was taxed. My family made me their target and did everything they could to keep me quiet at all costs. So many times I wanted to stop, to deny every memory, betraying myself to believe a different, kinder story. But each time this courage would kick in and take over. It was the only way through. I could not go around this mountain to get to the top.

Self-pity is a strong persuasion. It would derail my mission, make me a failure – a victim. I would fight the enemy of feeling sorry for myself time and time again.

Did I go back for the love of my children? That was a very strong goal to survive the attack that recovery would bring for sure, but it wasn't enough either. Many people have told me to stop telling this story because it just needs to be forgotten. I've been bombarded by well-intentioned folks telling me God wants me to put it behind me and live.

Sometimes forgetting just isn't enough. Sometimes forgetting the past can poison the present.

When my story stayed hidden, the weight was too enormous to bear. The older I got, the heavier it became. So, I began to tell what had happened to me.

As with all children, my deepest longing was to belong and to be loved. It was very simple. If I had told on my parents and exposed their deceit, I would have lost any hope of finding that. Of course, the fear of telling is yet another layer of dread. As I became a woman and had children of my own, I was confronted with a choice: stay in the denial I was taught, drag them along and pass down a generational deceit, or tell the truth. My love for them was deeper than any longing I had for myself. So, I began to tell my story in my early twenties.

It didn't go well. I had underestimated the battle that would ensue when I refused to drag my family's sin along with me on the cords of deceit. People hate the word sin, but what else do you call such debauchery? Incest is something not many want to talk about. And when you do, it's not welcomed. Oh, you can sit in a dark corner and share with someone else in a quiet secret. But, to announce to everyone this atrocity? Not so much! I found myself in a battle not just against my parents, but a battle of light and darkness. I needed tools that were outside of my strength to get through. Tools from a kingdom not of this world. I found those tools. I told my story. I'm still standing.

I can't change my history or bring a dead woman back to life, but I can tell the story to the best of my recall with full diligence to the truth, so help me God.

One

He Called Him Cholla

"You and I will always be unfinished business."
--Unknown

They were in love. My Dad and him. Or, at least, he with my father. Craig was Dad's best friend. As a child, I knew Craig better than I knew my own mother. Who knew if Dad ever loved him or my mom, but I know Craig adored my father. Craig proved that love through decades of time woven with deep loyalty to keep hidden their many crimes.

In my fifties, Craig was put into a nursing facility with early signs of dementia. I'd been to see Craig a few years earlier and he told me he was starting to become forgetful, so this came as no surprise. His nephew and wife were given the task of cleaning out his home and preparing it for sale. In his garage, under some heavy clutter and a toolbox, they found a letter. That letter was from me. I'd written to Craig years earlier asking him to help me close the murder case and return the buried woman to her family.

They emailed me and wanted to meet. I agreed. We talked for several long hours. It was difficult for all of us. His nephew bore a strong resemblance to Craig, which made my entire being uneasy. I quivered trying to rid myself of the panic attacks.

4

His eyes wore the same color as his uncle's but gave a warm depth of understanding. He carried himself with determination in his gentle walk and his hair fell deft like rabbit fur. The quiet tone of his words told me through story that he was trying to derail the unpleasant experiences he had dealt with from his father, Craig's brother. He told me he planned to never have children so his unpleasant, vile lineage would end with him. I assured him that he was nothing like his uncle -- explaining that Craig's glazed eyes imprinted on me and my siblings a category of man that you could not forget. He was not that.

A few days later, I received a call from his nephew's wife. She told me they had found a personal photo album that Craig had kept. The contents were a meticulous gathering of everything that mattered most to him. They'd found slews of other albums comprised only of landscape and nature photography, but this album was different. Very different. It held the most important people and moments of Craig's life – most prominently featuring my father. She told me that she could see their friendship was more than platonic. She was sure I'd find the evidence I needed to recover their secret bond.

Looking through the picture book it did prove something I knew long before: In 1955, two young boys hopelessly in love in a world that would not allow them to show it. The pictures produced a shrine or homage to their lives, and the mysteries and secrets they held together.

The album begins with the usual stuff, his parents, and grand-parents. Lots of pictures with his only sibling, a brother. A small smattering of things that mattered most to him, like the letter he wrote to Santa in 1947.

My story truly begins with them -- their bond, their love, their mayhem. And much of my story ends with them, unfortunately, and the secrets that each would take to his grave.

Page ten holds the first picture of my father. The inscription on the back says, "Stan in rope swing tree by valley apartments 1955."

My father is seventeen in this black and white picture. He's perched on the large limb of a tree, holding onto a thick rope that has several knots tied into it, almost in a Rapunzel type way. A burlap sack has been rolled up and tied in such a way as to lend a seat.

He looks handsome in his youthful innocence.

Then, another picture of Dad standing on the porch of an old, disheveled house in 1955. He has his arm around a woman. There's a small dog at her feet. My father seems to have the same outfit on that he did in the last picture. His face held no wrinkles and there was still a glow in his twisted smile.

A look I wouldn't see by the time I came around in 1964.

On the next page of the album is a trip where the boys go to Seaside, Oregon, in July of 1956. It's Craig and another friend named Sam. My father stayed close to Sam in his later years. I hadn't realized they'd been childhood friends. Sam was a thick man who was serrated with defiance – feeling his sharp-edged interior under his bold smile I kept my distance from his as a child but was intrigued.

Dad and Sam are both gone now, but this picture remains of a friendship that endured.

Next came another photo of Dad sitting on a large rock, the beach at his feet, with one foot slightly cocked into the sand. He's drinking Pepsi. He always drank Pepsi, but not when I was a small child. His drink of choice was mostly beer. What events ultimately led my father to start drinking beer like water? I'm saddened when I see the innocence that these pictures could have held -- friends, a beach trip. But, with these three sluggards, there was surely mayhem. I knew these men.

In another picture they stop on the side of the road to mess around, pretending strength in pushing over a tree. Innocent fun, right?

Then, a few more pictures of family and a picture or two of snow blizzards.

This book obviously stored everything that mattered to this man. Evidenced next by a landmark, his graduation picture. On the back he'd written, "High school graduation June 1957 north side of house at 4004 Columbia St." These teenagers were from the same small town, same small school.

Then the love story continued.

Craig is 6'5", thin and awkward. My father is a slight-framed 5 foot, 7 inches, devilish looks that add to his charm. Dad is wearing a captain's hat and looks as if he's dressed as a sailor. Craig is dressed in all white and has hints of a seaward weathered sailor himself. I learned later that he enlisted in the Navy, maybe the reason for these copycat threads. They're standing in front of a totem pole, slightly leaning in toward each other and both displaying huge grins. On the back of the picture, "Stan Steele and I. Tumwater. Summer of 57."

Summer of '57 -- reminded me of the love affair between Danny and Sandy in the movie *Grease.* The budding of a loving relationship.

The very next picture I'd already seen. I knew it very well.

In my forties, I went to see my father. By this time that was a very rare occasion. I walked into his house and followed the path to his private domain. A garage that had been turned into a type of family room. The room was his. Ashtrays, cigarettes, booze, and the stench of betrayal permeated the place.

There, on the wall above his chair, blown up into a much bigger proportion, was the very same picture that I now find in Craig's private album. It appears to be the original of that copy my father had hanging.

Why was this picture so significant to the two of them?

They're standing in front of a '41 Buick. On the back Craig has written,

"Stan Steele and I near Cascade Locks. Summer of 57 – Stan's 41 Buick."

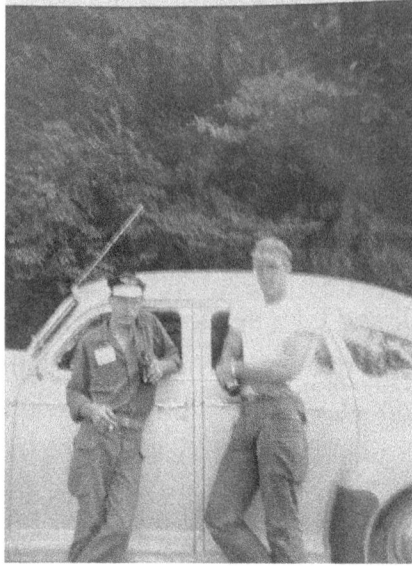

Was it their bond that the picture encapsulated for each of them? Again, that summer of '57.

On the next page are two graduation pictures. One of them is my dad, the other a friend named Cruz.

My father's picture has a handwritten name in the upper left corner. My father had inscribed the picture to Craig with a nickname. In all caps the word ---- CHOLLA. The bottom righthand corner is "Stan '57," in rememberable quotes.

My father's hair appears darker than normal, greased, and slicked back into a perfect 1950's hairdo. His face so young. I realize, again, this side of my father would be gone by the time I came around. Still, youth could not hide the all-pervading stare of his eyes. They were the same. Evil crept beneath the layer of this teenage fun. A slight grin hid his darkness.

He's wearing a suit with a button-up shirt and looks like a man beginning to hit the world with confidence. My heart broke a little with what could have been his.

I turned the picture over and recognized my father's handwriting. He wrote to Cholla:

> To a swell guy who has gotten me out of some jams that I couldn't have done. May a woman never break us up. Best of luck. Your buddy, Stan.

Underneath Stan is a diamond symbol. Under the diamond symbol my father writes his signature -- R E B.

Their reign of terror had already begun. These jams were an initiation, if you will, of Cholla into my father's well-orchestrated kingdom. The writing wasn't on the wall, it was on the back of an image.

The next graduation picture given to Craig was from Rick. The sentiments written on the back were:

Cholla! Best of luck to one of the biggest studs in Vancouver. Take her easy on the chicks, and I'll try to be around when they promote you to head janitor at wards. See you in California.

Cholla! They both called Craig Cholla.

They weren't planning on being separated by a woman, although cryptically they had written that into their words. They were meeting in California next.

This small journey through his picture book took me through these boys' formative high school years, but this was just the beginning.

My Dad got married on April 19, 1958.

The next photo was a picture of Craig, his brother, and granddad. He was home on leave from the Navy in "April 1958."

Did he return to go to my mother and father's wedding, or did he return to stop it?

Five more pictures were in the album, but none of them were with my father.

Then, exactly two years later, April 19, 1960, my parents' wedding anniversary, there is a picture of my father fishing with Craig. Craig has written a note, this time on the front of the picture, "Stan Steele at Salmon Creek 4-19-60."

Clearly, based on these dates, these two were never separated by a woman. In fact, they'd found a way to stay together despite his marriage. Nothing was enough to separate them. The bifurcation of the three did not happen. Rather, they became intertwined.

The storybook continues with two large photos of Craig's dad. A beer in each hand, a huge smile in one and a lit cigarette in his mouth in the next. About this time, his father committed suicide. Craig was the one who found him -- dead.

Six more pictures. Craig's picture novel continued, and the plot of my story had now become more complicated. My mother would lose my father to no one. Sharing him would be fine.

A professional photograph taken at the *Stardust* in Las Vegas, Nevada, is of my dad, Craig, and my mother. Dated December 7, 1964. They'd taken a road trip together. The three of them. This night the show was *Le Lido De Paris*.

I was five months old.

I knew this picture very well, too. It had been displayed in my parents' house for years. The funny thing was -- Craig had been cut out of it. That was the very last picture Craig ever put in this album of my father or mother. The album ended with Dad's obituary on December 8, 2010.

What happened during the missing forty-six years? Their relationship lived on through their deeds of darkness and the unfinished business they'd left behind.

My father, Craig, and my mother. The band of thieves had been created and the quantum jump into rape, murder, and pedophilia was just a few steps away. . .

Two

Delaware Lane

"I speak into the silence. I toss the stone of my story into a vast crevice; measure the emptiness by its small sound."
—*In The Dream House* by Maria Machado

In the summer of 1968, we lived on a small tree-lined street called Delaware Lane, the name reminiscent of a place where families live, and children play freely. But my home symbolized nothing of the sort. I grew up with two older sisters, Karen and Crissy, and one brother, Claude. We shared cookies, dinner, sodomy, rape, and baths together.

My oldest sister was the embodiment of the eldest child. Over-burdened with duty, she lacked luster for life and her thick, dark hair gave no shine – synonymous with her personality. She chose to be regimented and cruel -- loving the control she had over us. Maybe that helped her escape the pain of our daily existence.

Crissy was the middle child and like all of us, was slightly unkept. Her thin blonde hair as unruly as her pain. It seemed she had the thinnest skin of all of us. Her appearance always alluding to the help she longed for and needed; weak and frail she seemed lonely and afraid. Mom told me that she would cry uncontrollably for hours as a small child and she never knew what to do. Mom said it was very disturbing.

God, the poor thing, what she needed was protection, but she wasn't going to find it with them. She was my favorite.

Claude was my partner in crime. Brothers are synonymous with play and curiosity. Claude somehow felt limp and hallowed to me, which left a want in me to protect him. He was two years older, but I had some agility that he did not. I remember the dank smell of his bedroom when were teenagers, but he was almost odorless as a kid. He had a mean streak that he dramatized through me. His bond to only my mother would ultimately be his demise. Wanting to rescue him was a theme born between us – until it was not.

Claude and I kept an attitude that surpassed our dismal beginnings. We played together -- a lot. We made strange concoctions in the kitchen with no recipes to entertain ourselves. It seemed we could move outside of the box we were given and find moments of happiness. My father was extraordinarily cruel to my brother, and I hated watching their interactions. Maybe that's why I gave so much to him. When my brother tried to stand up for himself, my father's rage shut him down reminding us we had only rights in his house and no privileges.

Oh, but I also remember the sounds on our streets. Children laughing and the happy sounds of the ice cream man -- the man who peddled so much joy. Running down that transient source of cheeriness, I heard the sound coming down our lane, a street that can still reckon desire in me. He was coming, but I had to find money to get him. He wouldn't stop without the wave of a dollar. I had a fair sense of what a dollar was and knew I could find them in my mother's wallet. Tenacity was a courage that kept me going in those days. If I didn't display some grit, life would have taken me out, so off I went exploring. It wasn't difficult because my mother was easy, her habits unchanging. She kept her purse in the same spot. Her eyes always looked the same – dull and distant -- and her hair was always piled on top of her head like some sort of trophy. Her breath remained the same sickening smell of a woman who would take what she wanted at any cost. At last, I discovered the green slip that would stop the man with the music and put into my hands the small pleasure I so desperately needed to bring a moment's relief to my dismal world. I told him what I wanted, and he handed me an ice cream bar. I remember the day well. Somebody listened to a request I had. However small that deed was, I liked it– maybe more than the taste of that cold, sweet treat. As the ice cream dribbled down my hand, I couldn't help my mind wandering to the satisfying nature of being seen.

Our little house had a sliding glass door that led to another outside haven -- the backyard. It was nice out there. Grass you could run on, a swing set that gave hours of play, and a wooden fence to peer through. Although I don't remember much about the lady who lived on the other side of the wooden fence, I sure remember my family discussing the size of her body. She was a very large women and it made my parents feel better about themselves to shame her through their mockery. I choose to recall the laughter and the warmth of the sun's rays beaming across my back as I played. It was a place I could roam undisturbed – well, at least for a while.

I tried to stay out there if they'd let me. There was still light. Light to play by. Light to sing by. Light to be safe under. Why go inside? There was darkness in there. Who, in their right mind, would leave the swings for food? I always thought we should just play there...for a long, long while, held in the arms of the sun's warm comfort.

My father was the master of our interior -- they called it our home. On his forearm, in simple black ink, was a tattoo of the confederate flag with the letters R E B forged under it. His bloodline needed to be remembered and the indelible lettering under his skin assured that for him. Rebel – it was everything I knew him to be. Some kind of product of the '50s. Pegged Levis wore his thin frame. His white t-shirt embodied the man who spoke with a slow, Southern drawl. Rolled up in his sleeve was often a pack of Winstons -- the red box. Dad loved Johnny Cash, but he loved chaos and control more. My father would drink until his legs betrayed him and he was forced to give in, subdued only until his strength returned.

My mother, by her own confession, had too many children. There were four of us. I was the caboose and, unfortunately, was the one she wanted least. Through the years, she'd been sure to make me aware of the discomfort my life brought to her. She told me she spent the least amount of time with me as an infant. "I ain't mad at nobody," Woody Guthrie once wrote, but I sure had a knife in my soul from the time that she conceived me.

My parents were a good-looking couple. After four children, my mother touted a svelte figure and wore snug clothing to enhance her outward appeal, proving her worth to my father. Father needed no form of flattery. He knew how to take what he wanted when he wanted it. Mother worked continuously, fearing the poverty she came from. Dad could have cared less about a career. He was lazy and wanted someone else to do the work. He'd rather take than give. His half-dressed body slumped in a chair, supported his unkept thick dark hair. His mind focused on gluttony, over drinking and satisfying his need to control. Most days he wandered around in a T-shirt and his jeans unbuttoned. He was always home in those days perched with a beer in his hand demanding something from anybody.

From the outside looking in, our home was small but nothing different than ordinary. They threw parties at the house on the weekends. Now they both were dressed to the nines, hair perfect and smiles firmly in place. We had lots of people, music, dancing, and fun. We only got to watch from down the hall, but they were happy, it was clear.

When the parties were over, the drunkenness remained. Not just a drink here or there, or an occasional party -- it was full blown, bastardly alcoholism. It crept into every crevice. You could not hide from its influence. In the morning, Dad drank red beers. He showed me the trick of what salt looked like filtering through the colored brew.

In the morning time my father was unusually quiet, maybe even subdued –likely nursing a hangover. Bare-chested, head hung low; he'd crack his first beer. Wanting him to be pensive of his bad behavior, I surrounded him in my longing to be held and to watch him -- believing somehow if I stayed close to him, I could find a measure of protection. Mom had usually left for work by the time we got up, off to a job that consumed most of her time and all her energy. She was not going to be poor again. When she was home, Father always needed her attention – well, commanded her attention. Chapped by life's rejections he was an unsustainable manic. Knowing his tactics, I stayed close. Sometimes his scalding aggression flew around me to another kid.

Maybe it was the alcohol, maybe he was just ready to stir the pot, but the air always changed when it was about to happen. He paced, like some force within him began to thaw and then stir. You didn't dare disturb this disgruntled varmint. He'd rise and come find you. He didn't need any help. The day would become about him. Solely. Completely. Relentlessly about him. That was the beauty of our mornings.

I'd be lost in happy play with my brother. Dad would enter with that slight smile and a cocky look in his eye. Always hoping for attention, and knowing I really didn't have a choice, I would go to him. Occasionally, he'd hold me gently and tell me he loved me. I was his most precious possession. He would try to assure me that he wouldn't hurt me, he'd coax me into believing that if he'd ever hurt me before he was sorry, he'd plea how he needed me, loved me, and that I loved him too. He made me feel like I alone made his life worth living. He didn't like to take from you if he believed you were unhappy with him, so he worked at getting you to the place where you were receptive, and he could take your love. He didn't want your rejection; his being was already saturated with that.

So, as soon as my unconditional response was in place, he'd begin his attack with the viciousness of a vulture.

My mind screamed, "I knew it!"

Trust was nowhere to be found.

Trapped in this vulnerable cycle with him, my thoughts churned for new answers. Outrunning him was impossible. Staying close to him didn't give enough to quiet his inner beast. No protective wall would stand against him.

My mother was different – she didn't seem to want anything from me but my absence.

We had a corner piece of a sectional couch in our living room, which sat next to the floor-to-ceiling brick fireplace and was surrounded by stark mid-century furniture. It was a pleasant gray pink. I loved the color of that couch and remember it with vivid recall from sustained memorization during these sexual attacks. My father took me and laid me down in the middle piece of the sectional. I had a dress on. Dad positioned himself in front of me and got on his knees. Fire literally seemed to appear in his eyes as he readied himself. His moves seemed so precise in the middle of complete chaos. His arm flexed as his hand moved toward me.

My mind seemed to scream out loud, "No, don't choke me!"

I'd fought too much, and he needed to keep me still. I felt his grip grow stronger around my tiny neck. It didn't take much with the strength of his hands on a three-year-old's throat. The only focus I had now was to gasp for air. A blackness entered my mind, and it shocked me. I didn't understand that I was close to passing out but finding air was my only desire now. I did not understand his hate for me. Where was his fury rising from? Trying to struggle against his actions was no help at all. It was never going to end! Then, my body felt pierced with an excruciating pain. The outbursts of anguish that rushed out of me were unmercifully ignored.

Almost as abruptly as it started, it had finally ended. My limbs were feathery and light from the brutish attack as I walked back to my room. Having no understanding about virginity and such things, it would take decades to heave through the intoxicating journey of pain. All I knew right then was that my body wept from the inside out and there was razor-sharp pain everywhere.

What had I done so wrong? Why was I being punished? Why did he hate me? I tried very hard to be a good girl for him. None of that seemed to matter. He stole the most precious gifts I had to offer.

He then banished me to my room until I could get my body to stop throbbing, my crying dismissed, and my demeanor under control. You know, the craziest piece to this whittled-down nightmare is that when the winds of destruction stop, and you've pulled yourself together, life returns to what seems normal. When I focused on denying my feelings, my composure would return, and my placid smile would put itself firmly in place.

Then, and only then, could I rejoin the family.

Three

Indoctrination

"But I think I know so well the pain we children clutch to our chests, how it lasts our whole lifetime, with longings so large you can't even weep. We hold it tight, we do, with each seizure of the beating heart: This is mine, this is mine, this is mine."

—*My Name Is Lucy Barton* by Elizabeth Strout

Dad taught me, lesson after lesson, to artfully survive. He busied himself with menial work when he wasn't abusing. His hands crusted with years of conniving and nails darkened by cigarettes. He was a ready teacher. Controlling my emotions and implementing denial was the first weapon he gifted me for my arsenal of psychological tools. Denial became my gift as a child. Trust? A fucking joke. Trust lived nowhere near our street and never came inside our home. You must choose which voice to listen to as a child. That's what it really boils down to. Who do I believe? Not, who do I trust. Not in houses like mine.

Denial was a gift straight from the throne of God. I wouldn't have endured without it. The unreasoning web that my parents had built had no consideration for its construction other than to entrap. It was meant to have no way out. Lunacy is probably built in this way. To stay out of the destructive voices I found in my parents, I used the tool they gave me. It was my God-given right that was now mine. And I am thankful for it.

Today, I've learned that I don't need this tool anymore, but I certainly did at one time. I'm grateful it was available to me. The images of body parts I couldn't unsee, the smell of an old motel room that I couldn't stop, the sound of a strange scream – experiences that were in a constant projectile made it impossible to tolerate more than simply getting through it all. To sustain the memories then would have been a demand too tall for my little frame. Withholding it all from memory was my gift to survive. Contradiction was my gift to allow play. Disagreement with reality my gift so I could sleep. Oh, the truth still happens every now and again, but at least for many uncalibrated moments, I got to breathe.

These tools handed down ultimately became weapons I would use against my father. I developed some of my own tools as well. I stayed constantly vigilant in my observation of him, memorizing the way he exerted control and manipulated others to get what he wanted. I was a soldier being indoctrinated for war. Mundane family projects became training opportunities for surviving the battleground of childhood.

One summer day, the family was enlisted to clean the garage. Being the youngest, I'm not sure how much I had to do with the cleaning, but I rode my trike up to see what was going on. Just about to garner a view of the activity, a large rock was hurled my way. It connected with my forehead and knocked me off my perched position onto the ground.

Dazed by the rock, I was terrified. Blood was streaming down my face, and I froze.

My mind questioned, "Was this something I'd seen before?"

I was in a trauma-shock response when they brought me to my heartless mother. Tragically my mind came to no good conclusion when she lifted me up to look. She never wanted me and the disturbed look she gave me for interrupting her was obvious. My hope for comfort dashed. She placed me on the counter in the laundry room and some awful smelling stuff was wiped all over my wound. Then, it was determined that my bleeding forehead was serious enough to get to the hospital to have it looked at. I'd never been to a hospital before or anywhere for any kind of outside help. This was new territory. Admittedly, I was a bit scared.

It was my father's great privilege to pretend to be like a caring father and drive me there. No one in our house ever wanted to inconvenience themselves for such a menial waste of time. We took his old blue truck and away we went.

The hospital was old and decrepit, the halls extraordinarily tall with a ceiling as high as the sky. New places didn't scare me. I liked the adventure. I was safer outside of my home than in it. But the antiseptic aroma matched the hollow feeling in the air. There was clear uncertainty of what would be next. I didn't like not knowing.

Passing a coined vending machine, Dad looked down at me and said, "Don't cry and I'll let you get some of those crackers." He wasn't nervous like I was. His calm demeanor told me he wanted this over quickly and without incident.

A prize! Oh, I wanted that prize but making my father happy was what I wanted most. Or was it that I didn't want his hatred. Not sure but I had already been taught how to control my tears when commanded to do so, so figured this would be achievable.

Taken into a large room they placed me on a cold metal table. A bright light hovered above the doctor, a nurse, and me. I really wanted my dad with me. I didn't feel pain, but I was scared. By this time in my life, I'd already been raped, seen rape and that seemed to eclipse the pain of this experience. And, that prize! A prize for being a good, quiet girl. Never receiving a reward before, I was delighted to get something good for being hurt. In the end, I received a few stitches to close the gap in my skin, but the pain was nothing. I had kept completely silent.

Returned to my dad, we began the procession down the hall, past the vending machine, and out to the car.

"Hey, wait!" I tugged on my father's hand and began to cry. Yep – now I cried. I didn't have to tell Dad what he'd forgotten, my tears reminded him.

He did comply and I received my just reward -- a reward for not showing any pain. My only comfort that day was the cellophane wrapped crackers. I stood beside my father on the bench seat of his blue truck, savoring those buttery wafers as if they were caviar and fine vodka given to me by a suitor. I was very proud of my achievement and my reward that day. Dad never looked my way.

Five months after the murder, we moved from our small home in the city to our completed habitat deep in the mountains. Our closest neighbor was miles away. I cannot fathom how it must have felt for me to be moved onto the land where we had so heinously and recently tossed this woman's body. It chills me even now.

Left behind in the city were our friends and those magical sidewalks that brought me such joy. Dad decided he'd exchange the ice cream man for the dark shadows that danced in the forest just beyond the parameter of safety in our new land. To keep watch over this fortress, Father enlisted the protection of a Doberman pincher. The dog was well trained and motivated by fear. He was beautiful, and yet you could see an agitation that was right beneath the skin – just like his owner. I still carry with me a scar on my right eyebrow from his gnarly bite.

Mom and Dad continued to throw parties at their new digs, but they now lasted the length of an entire weekend – probably due to our remote location and their appetite for lust. It agitated the dog to have strangers in our home, so he was placed in the laundry room to keep the guests out of harm's way. I wanted to go be with him. Although Dad wasn't home, the dog closely represented his interests when he was away. I was four years old when I opened the door, during one of these marathon parties, straight into the line of fire of his jagged teeth. It felt like his mouth swallowed my face. Tears raced for my neck as the fear and pain of the encounter left me shaken. Walking up to my mom in the kitchen was something I hated doing, but I had to. She was cooking for our guests – her favorite way to earn favor. Strangers gave more to her ego than any of us could.

She cleaned up the blood and called my dad to tell him what happened. He was the one in charge of me -- my emotions, my pain, my very existence. Dad was over at his cousin's house in Bear Prairie (another perverted hick) and it would take some time for him to get home. Mom sat me down on the cold, stone hearth of our roman brick fireplace and told me Dad was on his way. She returned to the kitchen to keep cooking for our guests.

I couldn't go to the elementary school in my home district when I first started kindergarten. The school only offered half-day classes and that would have left me home alone for much of the day. As my guardian angel would have it, Mom decided to take me to my maternal grandmother's for the school year.

Back where there were porches and sidewalks. I liked it there. People were all around and that meant safety. Grandma would send me out the door and I'd walk the five or so blocks to my elementary school. This time with my grandmother had proven to be a safe space in my childhood that altered my life for the good. When I'd stroll back to her house through the umbrella of branches that hovered just above my reach on the streets back to her house, she'd be waiting for me.

Each day she would make me what she lovingly called our *special lunches.* Those lunches were always an anticipated delight – a gift every day. She served us both on two oddly colored green plates; one plate had a hand-painted figure of a man, and the other was adorned with a lovely woman. Each plate had three distinct sections and each section held a small, wonderful treat for me. Often, there'd be a quarter of a sandwich in the largest section, three olives in the next, and a piece of celery stuffed with cream cheese in the last. I adored these lunches with this special lady.

My grandmother was teaching me just as my father was. His skills were harsh and cruel. My grandmother taught me how to survive in a different way. With true strength and dignity. Not denying the truth but standing up to it. She was small but mighty in her way. We found things to do to bide our time. She taught me card games. We strolled down the sidewalk together holding hands. Her front porch swing swayed to the cadence of her love as she petted my hand. I watched her pick Concorde grapes from her backyard and then boil them to release their sweet fragrance. After they cooled, she dumped them into a pillowcase. She carefully tied the pillowcase to her bedroom door-knob, placed a bowl under the sac and we gathered the juice that bled through.

This warm year with my grandmother built a bond between us that lasted her lifetime -- and beyond. It also gave me just enough resiliency to survive my childhood. I could fill another book with stories of just hers. She rode motordrome on an Indian motorcycle at the bowery of Coney Island in the '20s. She would tell me stories of how she closed the floorshows in those days with a special dance she created to "My Song of India." When I was a teenager, my grandmother told me I had Sisu. This is a Finnish concept described as a stoic determination, tenacity of purpose, grit, bravery, resilience, and is held by Finns themselves to express their national character. She gave that to me. Those words that she spoke to me that day standing in her driveway are alive and strong in my moral fiber.

Later in life, after my grandmother had been moved into a retire-ment facility and had to leave her home of over fifty years, I hatched a plan that was inspired by a book called Tuesdays with Morrie by Mitch Albom. The subtitle is: An old man, a young man, and life's greatest lesson. The book chronicles their time together, through which Mitch shares Morrie's lasting gift with the world. I asked her if there was a book she'd read that she would like us to now read together. She said that there was a book she read in her twenties. It was called I Wasn't Born Yesterday. That was all she knew.

I found that book in an old bookstore thousands of miles away. It is an anonymous autobiography as told to Rivkin and Spiegelgass. The woman in the story lived in Coney Island but traveled the world and had a very colorful life. The book was published in 1935 and has a language of its time:

"Stop mooning," Big Jerry said to me one afternoon." You think I'm going to let you sit on your big fat can while I dish out the coin? You got work to do, baby. You got to start making a living."

While I read to my grandmother, she would stop me from time to time. She would say, "They're talking about the Virginia Reel, a roller-coaster on Coney Island." Another time she would tell me, "There was the Park Luncheonette on that corner."

Nothing would take our bond.

During my first year of school, my mom would drive us down the mountain and into the town where my grandmother lived. It took us some twenty-five to thirty minutes to make the drive. I wanted desperately to have my mother's attention because I was already certain I didn't have her love. We pulled up to a stop sign and the right turn would take us into town.

Clearly, if Mom was going to give me some attention, she would have. So, I'd been considering a plan. I'd open the glove box compartment and use the door as my prop. I began playing a concerto with my little fingers hitting the imaginary keyboard before me. My brother was her favorite and he got piano lessons. She looked over. I was thrilled but had only captured her for a few seconds. Her look was a clear signal to me – stay quiet and keep away from her. I needed to keep my pain to myself -- and I did.

I told my mom that story when I was an adult, and do you know that she remembered it, too? Then, she added, "I did see that you were a troubled little girl, but" she paused, "I didn't know what to do with your pain."

She was never there. The nights I woke up and ran hot baths because my leg pain was intolerable, or when I'd have to go to their room because of night terrors I could not calm. I asked her as an adult if she ever heard the bathwater running. She told me she had. She just didn't have time for my pain.

She didn't miss my pain because she'd been the orchestrator of much of it.

Sometimes, Mom dropped us off at a babysitter's house and then went to her very important job that would build the esteem she so desperately sought. I remember the tin-colored anodized aluminum cups this nanny served our morning milk in. On special occasions, we got Strawberry Nesquik to stir into our milk – milk that was so cold it made your teeth hurt. The house had a creep factor to it, and oftentimes, I didn't want to be there. Once, I began to cry uncontrollably, so much so that the babysitter had to call my mother to come get me. I was elated that Mom would soon be on her way. That babysitter walked into the cold bedroom and told me to get out of bed. She briskly sat me down in a chair in the living room to await my mother's arrival.

Mom gathered and placed me in the front seat of the car and promptly drove me to my grandmother's house. I always wanted her to look in my eyes. I felt if she looked, she would see me. She was upset with me because she had to leave work to tend to such a silly, troubled girl. She was always upset with me.

I needed to tell her about the boy who called to me in the babysitter's basement. But she didn't have time for such nonsense.

About the age of five or six, I started burying myself, or more accurately, my pain, in addiction. Sounds far-fetched, right? Nope. Food was everywhere and easily accessible.

One night my mom prepared for a weekend party. Food was being set up in a welcoming format for the guests and my siblings and I would be banished upstairs when they showed up. I would slink to the tables and sneak food. This night I ate so much that when we were sent upstairs and I went to bed, I vomited it all up all. I was aghast. I hadn't realized how much I'd ingested. This addiction wouldn't stop until years later, when I would find new vices to replace the old.

My dad told me often that my food addiction came from the year I stayed with my grandmother. He desperately wanted and needed to break that bond my grandmother had built with me. It gave me strength and he knew it. He did not like her resilience and he did not want me to know her skills. She too was cunning and knew how to manipulate. Her strength in needing little from anyone was power.

We had ordinary times as well. Dad was an auto-body repairman in a local body shop. He told me he liked painting cars but couldn't perfect painting without runs so he stayed on the Bondo side of the business.

He tuned his radio into a bible station that piped biblical content out loud in the body shop where he worked. He used to tell us how his co-workers would comment on his "Jesus' station." He wanted everyone to know about this new portrayal he'd created. He seemed well-liked and now discriminated against for his faith (barf!).

Mom was in the first group of students through a new court-reporting school that opened in the '70s in a large city nearby. We were the typical middle-class family: nice home, new cars, and Mom (a few times) canning in the kitchen.

We played as children do. My brother and I were close – albeit with sexual overtones. We pretended and explored a lot together. This was the early '70s so there wasn't much going on inside the house in the way of electronics, so you had to create your own fun. One time we scratched out a detailed menu for my parents with an imaginary restaurant running in our home kitchen. Mom and Dad were our first customers. It was fun! Our parents graciously played the roles we gave them, and it was good. If we lived in the house with the attitude of "things are fine and your pain isn't showing," we seemed to get along just fine.

One thousand eight hundred and ninety-five days after the murder, our fake family made headlines. My father murdered on June 8, 1968, we adopted a little boy and appeared in the local paper on August 26, 1973. The riddle of my family couldn't have been scripted. No person could have unraveled the demonic turmoil they hid.

In this newspaper article, my mother says, "Another boy was 'just right' for the farm-like setting. We had a lot out here to share with a boy like Jimmy." The article continues, "The adoption agency had been quite specific in describing Jimmy's speech and emotional problems. Jimmy is talking in complete sentences now, but only when asked to do so. Previously, he communicated with one word at a time, or meaning-less 'baby talk.'"

What the fuck was this family doing adopting an abused child? Their house was already filled with abused, unwanted children.

The family was now subjected to the tedious adoption process, which brought county caseworkers into our home for close inspection. We had been trained well and we passed easily with flying colors. Can you imagine if the caseworker had known about the body buried in the dump just a few football lengths away from our house?

The newest addition to our fraudulent family affair was Johnny. Part American Indian, he had been abandoned in a motel room as a baby and had been in foster care ever since. He came with a disclaimer that he was a troubled little boy. It was obvious when you met him – his eyes lost in a distant place. His eyes, skin, and hair were dark. He was a darling little boy. His soul deafened by desertion; he gave little notice to anything.

Weren't we just the pillar of our community to help this little guy?

The local newspaper ran a story about our extended hands. It was a full-page article with a photo of Mom standing in the kitchen canning peaches. Three of us were lined up on our oversized couch, my brother and I glowing with on-demand, placid smiles, my oldest sister is not in the picture and my middle sister showed signs of depression on her pained face. Mom had that article buried in boxes at her house. It's proof to her, after all, that we really were a good family.

Only a few years later, that little boy was returned to the state. Our parents told us it was because he had no conscience and they feared for our safety. I don't know the truth of that story, nor do I really care. Dad and Mom surely couldn't help him. Dad said we needed him so my brother wouldn't be gay like my mom's brother was. That, of course, didn't make it into the newspaper article either.

Sometime during these years, Mom and Dad found religion. That was all our house needed: another disguise. What my father represented was anything but the Jesus of the bible. He was a wolf in sheep's clothing. Mom loved this new part of Dad. A much cleaner representation of the beast that still lingered inside him.

When I went to see Craig in my fifties, we chatted about this godly conversion. Craig laughed and put his head down slightly and said, "The last time I saw Stan, he was still the same Stan I knew."

Dad told me a story one day in my teenage years. We were driving down the mountain to the local corner store. Dad and I talked often and by now I had developed the ability to derive some peace listening to his lies. He recalled a morning when he woke up on the property with a bad hangover. He said he woke up, lit a cigarette, and walked outside. He heard a car drive by on the isolated road in the distance. He said that he wanted to be free like the person in that car. He assumed that person hadn't murdered and wasn't a pedophile. He envied the stranger who didn't have a throbbing head and hell in his heart.

Coincidentally, this was the morning he'd decide to go to rehab. He went into a local in-house program a few days later. We all went and visited him as a united front because we were such a strong family.

That very possibly was the only time my father was "clean and sober." For many years after, he just hid his drinking. About a decade or less later, his drinking started to show again. His new religion didn't create a change but brought a much deeper deception because it gave him and Mom a smooth cover. Their anger wasn't gone. Their hatred was alive and well. He and Mom were still raging pedophiles and continued to sexually abuse me into my teen years. Their manipulations were weapons of defense for every relationship they had, and religion was just another piece to the game.

On their new pretend journey, my parents commenced this phony procession by attending bible study every Wednesday evening. My two older sisters were now in their teens, Claude a preteen and I was most likely 8 or 9. My sisters I barely knew by now. The years of destruction, chaos and control had isolated all relationships to dissociated caves far away from each other but for the sharp-edged attacks that came from my brother. They all somehow believed that my father's over-attention to me was the favor they wanted. Did they forget the high cost of his time?

Any time my parents were away from the house, it was game on. Freedom! My two sisters had invited a couple of neighbor boys in. After the air had been ornamented with thunderous music spinning from the turntable, the lights were dimmed and they all disappeared, five years younger than my oldest sister, I was quite intrigued and a little scared (I was always scared). I needed to stay unseen and spy. The girls were just having fun with the boys -- a very natural thing for teen girls to do.

Without warning, Mom and Dad came home early from bible study. Somebody noticed the car pulling in the driveway and shouted, "They're home!" The girls fearfully sprang into frantic action. Lights were being turned back on, the music halted, and the boys ran out the back door half dressed in deliria. The silence deafening waiting for Dad to walk through the door. My father held an omniscience, and we knew it. You couldn't hide much from him living in that house. His shadow followed you everywhere, intermingling with you to the point of not knowing which one was you anymore. My mother, his eager adjutant, would help him in his scurry to control. He walked with the determination of a rat hunting cheese.

As a conniving scavenger would, he found a pair of male boots on the back patio, outside the laundry room door. I stayed close to his tail, knowing that was the safest place right now. I was the teacher's pet and my siblings hated me for that, but I knew how to stay safe. I didn't want him to think I had anything to hide -- that I had somehow betrayed him as they had.

He found my sister showering in the upstairs bathroom. He flew through the door and peeled back the shower curtain. My sister clutched the curtain, trying to cover herself. My dad procured a belt he used "just to keep us in line;" a leather belt studded with metal rivets. It left an angry trail of welts in its wake.

He tore it off and began beating her nude body -- whipping any sign of rebellion out of her. She sobbed and cried out for one of us to help her. She clung desperately to the shower curtain to both hide her naked body and to steady herself against the force of his blows. He grotesquely lashed out again and again. Finally, she could hold on no longer and slipped, falling into the tub, ripping the shower curtain down as she tumbled. I had already seen her wet legs distorted with bloody welts and I couldn't watch any longer.

Yeah, he was a changed man all right.

To find moments of safety in a house riddled with chaos, I created a desk area in my closet. We had some built-in shelving that was meant to hold clothes. To construct this inviolable shelter, I moved all the clothes to one shelf. Next, I turned the empty shelf over to make a flat surface for writing and drawing. I had created a world away from the rest. I put in a lamp and stocked my makeshift desk with crayons and paper. I'd draw my way into a different, kinder world and hide from the evil that never left that house. This was part of the skill of survival that I taught myself. Dad did not like independence or separation of any kind, so I had to find moments away that were only mine. No fear. No pain. Nothing but time to breathe.

Mom and Dad taught us how to skillfully manipulate situations. We learned that if you wanted something, merely take it. If they wouldn't let go, apply anger, outbursts, rage. I understood the art of it all. They were good teachers and reinforced their art through demonstrative techniques so we wouldn't forget their power.

In my early teens, I was awoken with a blunt compression on the side of my bed. It was my father. He loosely slipped under the covers with me and began a distorted make-out session. This wasn't something he normally did. Pretend lovers -- some inscribed Lolita moments. It was revolting. My damaged vagina was used once again.

My mother must have been aware of this because now it seemed she was demanding her time in a blasted trio. I was being called to their bedroom. It'd been a long time since that train had come. I'd like to see this as a form of punishment she believed I had coming. Taking my place on their pedestal bed I waited for instruction.

Reeling that filthy memory forward, my father is calling me back into his room. My anus throbbing from pain and the nauseating smell from my mother's vagina forced me to run to the toilet and vomit. Dad was angered that his engorged gluttony had to wait.

When I returned, his bestiality continued with more force, clinching my sides tightly with his hands as my body recoiled and seemed

impenetrable. His desperation paid off and his pleasure wasn't interrupted again. There was a grace that day -- Mother did not receive hers.

About this time my mother started a teen Christian support group
in our home for my friends. Not recalling the name of the book, it was
about grooming yourself and nurturing things now that we were becoming young woman. Two of my friends came – one time. Their faces
watched my mother's action as she shared, a concerned mother helping
budding girls become woman. Her pinky slightly rose as she spouted
her knowledge of care. Her thick blonde hair kept slightly unruly but
groomed and the slight sheen to her racy red lipstick portrayed a
woman who knew. Who was she?

These prigs had not changed.

Four

Daddy's Angel

"Here is the world. Beautiful and terrible things will
happen. Don't be afraid."
—Beyond Words by Frederick Buechner

Love in our home was my father's design. It somehow swirled the
colors of hatred and love together so tastefully you were hard pressed
to tell the difference. But the cunning language he proudly crafted
seemed poorly thought out, its unpredictability often undermining
his systematic ruling. Nothing was ever set in stone but precarious–
changing in an instant with a mood swing. My mother's love, too, was
at a minimum complicated. Mostly, she pursued my father's love and
that was a wicked game nobody could win. They both knew what they
wanted and used inappropriate means to gain it.

Like all of us in that household, I wanted to believe I was Daddy's
angel, his prized possession, and I'd be good enough to win that title.
Day in and day out, I retraced the steps of what my father wanted,
memorized them -- what he needed to feel loved and what he needed
to feel wanted. There was not a space written into the script for what
I wanted. I didn't see anything wrong with this at the time. It was the
only way I knew, and the way I liked it -- keeping his moods at bay by

serving him didn't feel that bad to me, although this did put me at odds with my mother.

When I was small, Dad sexually abused me in the living room, the bedroom – out in the trailer in our backyard – anywhere he wanted. With this continued code of conduct, where he was the dominating receiver and it was all about him, I could hide away. If I didn't require anything -- love, kindness, or attention then it felt like an escape hatch was available. A safe place to hide away. Needing something from him brought vulnerability and vulnerability was something that had to be squashed.

Keenly aware that I needed to stay distanced from my mother or she'd rule some form of punishment against me, I busied myself with nothing really. This was something I could manage. Keeping isolated as much as I could insulated me against the frigid air of her rejecting stabs.

His love wasn't my goal, and neither was hers. I already knew their definition of love and I wanted nothing to do with it. In fact, when Dad died, I told him I wasn't there for his love. I had learned to live without it. I had even learned to live without the hope of needing it. Dwight Yoakam said it best when he sang, "I ain't that lonely yet." I used to call that my signature song.

I basked often in this new river of denial. Dad broke my will and personality until I became almost nothing, with no will of my own. No identity. Then, he rebuilt me and shaped my will to match his.

No love in. No love out.

And I did get something back -- he didn't share his children with Craig anymore – Craig was long gone. Dad rarely asked much from you, except the occasional rape and one time sodomy to avoid impregnating me. If you didn't fall out of line in any way, you'd be spared most of his abuse. However, even a minor infraction had severe consequences. He would tell you to go up to his room and wait for him. It would take an hour or more before he'd arrive to administer the punishment. He'd walk in and tell you to take your pants down to your bare bottom. You'd have to lie over the bed, and he'd begin the hits. It could leave patches of blood but always left deep welts. All this to take away our belief that we had any freedoms. His rule was always: you have no rights, only privileges. We heard that rule often. He taught us that independence was wholly a part of rebellion. Period. And rebellion was not tolerated. Thinking independently was a crime in our home. A God-given gift that my father captured.

At about the age of eight, I settled into a kind of resolute existence with dissociation as my guide. Everything seemed blurred and hazy, yellow-clouded, illusive. Leg cramps would wake me at night -- many, many nights. Sometimes I would just get up, go to the bathroom, turn the light on and sit on the toilet. I had taught myself how to stare intently at one spot until I was floating outside of my body. I loved that feeling. Later, I was dumbfounded when I was told that my practice was classic dissociation.

Sleep brought little rest. The recurring nightmare continued to haunt me. I was even told by my brother that I sleep-walked outside in the early hours of the morning. I wasn't witnessing anyone being raped or murdered, so, I did my best to get onboard this new train that was now operating in our house.

Sometimes we'd watch movies and eat the best popcorn around. Dad adored buttery popcorn, so early on I learned how to master the popping of that stove-top treat. If I could bring in a bowl of pleasure to his liking, I was doing it -- receiving more small accolades of acceptance. I enjoyed these times of pretend family. Sitting next to my father and sharing movie time seemed more normal. He always wrecked it by picking an area on my leg, then slowly rubbing his fingers back and forth, like Chinese torture. I hated when he touched me! If I could have ripped his hand aside, I would have. Mostly, I just tried not to sit by him – which he rarely let happen.

My brother and I had remained close through the years, albeit I turned a blind eye to his sexual predator style with me. We spent hours in the woods on exploratory missions tracking trails of water, finding skeletal remains of some animal we couldn't determine, or playing in an imaginary home we'd built in the shadows of the trees. We called it our fort.

Life was better. In fact, life had so moved on that when my brother and I had to get groceries for our fort, where do you think we went? The dump on our land, of course. There wasn't anything you couldn't find on your imaginary grocery list. I had no fear of that garbage pit because I had no memory of the murder in the forefront of my mind, yet. My mind and body screamed the truth at me in the night hours, but during the day we lived Dad's new religion, wore his cloak of love and denial, and built a different outlook far from the truth.

Dad's training had left a new code hovering over my bones, a code that I was safe and that we were loved. The hardest card I would have to play against my father and mother in the future would be this false sense of love scripted by the Spirit of Religion. It was an addictive feeling that I knew well. Loyalty was demanded, but that was okay – it was all that I'd been taught. It was a much better than feeling rejection, and they were, after all, my parents. I loved them. They taught me that.

One night, long ago, my mother came into my room – frantic. I must have been a preteen or so. She told me I had to get up and go to my father. He was slipping into a diabetic coma from which he might never return. She was scared, I could hear it in her voice. She had tried to get my father to drink some glucose-laced orange juice, which would bring him out of his diseased state.

As my brother often said, "He's been dying since we were ten and I became the caretaker to his disease. He would not take the drink from her but insisted that I give it to him. Was this episode proof that he believed our love was different or just another manipulative maneuver to leverage control over me? I suspect my father, in his deranged way of thinking, believed the bond between us was special. I loved him, he knew, because after all that he did -- I remained by his side.

Life continued, and so did the odd order of normalcy. Our parents sat us all down as a family and told us that we got to choose how we would spend the family money. A choice? One in which we would be included. We could choose between a long road trip vacation or a *Games People Play* game room. I'll never forget the *Games People Play* carpet my mother described to us in detail.

Mom was never excited about anything, but she was excited about this makeshift playroom. Sitting on the floor in a circle with an air of excitement, we listened to her explain the details of the carpet. Mom was a dreamer, and we were listening to another of her fantasies. Dad and the rest of the family was bent on the family vacation around the United States. Did I say choice? It quickly became clear that it would ultimately be his choice.

Dad had a '70 Ford pickup, a perfect vehicle to load a camper onto and cart four children on a road trip around the contiguous United States. A small opening connected the inside of the camper to the inside of the truck cab and a black vinyl flap snapped in to join the two together. This way, Dad could maintain his discipline and always yell his commands during the excursion. Sometimes, when in trouble, we had to spend time in the cramped, smelly bathroom of the camper -- a great incentive to mind him well.

We had been on our journey for some time when Dad told us we would soon be arriving in Georgia, to visit his cousin, Christine. Christine had three children. He phoned her when we were a few days from her house. She explained that her two youngest children had just been murdered by her ex-husband and only she and her oldest daughter remained. What a somber visit that was! During the stay, I had to sleep with my aunt Christine. Above her bed was a door in the ceiling and I took notice of the latch that kept it shut.

Ominous panic ripped through my veins. Subconsciously, I already knew what murder was. It had only been four years since I had witnessed the slaying. My little brain went into havoc. I was a wreck. I had insomnia all night. I was so frightened that a body would be behind that door in the ceiling. My mind raced to find what would not return in memory to me for many years. Now, here I was, trying to get through this night with her children having just been slain. I said nothing of my anxiety to anyone. That was strictly forbidden by now – actually, it had always been forbidden.

Christine reconstructed the story. She and her ex had an ugly divorce. He threatened her often. One day, her oldest daughter had come to her with a compelling dream she'd had -- her father asked the three kids to go fishing with him. In the dream, the children never returned, but only three dead fish that were left on her mother's doorstep. When their father called and asked them to go fishing, she'd been so stricken and convinced by what the dream showed her, she refused to go. She was the only child who wasn't murdered.

Dreams do work if we listen. Maybe as I grew, the dreams that came to me in my twenties I heeded, because of this story. Sometimes life works as if we have angels guiding us.

We left her house and drove into Tennessee where Dad's family was from. The day before we arrived a boy had been killed in a knife fight on a bridge. No one seemed overly concerned -- it was the '70s in the South. I guess, as Dad explained it, knifings just weren't that uncommon. He was home, for sure. I didn't like the chill of the South, but I loved those chocolate sheet cakes. We loaded up and left Dad's birthplace. Our trip had taken us through forty-six additional states in about two months' time.

Which state Dad's bloodline had started in was quite clear.

Five

The Death of My Inner Child

"For truth is truth to the end of reckoning."
~ Measure for Measure by William Shakespeare

Surely, I had many dreams as a child, but I cannot remember one of them. Except the one that returned to me repeatedly. I wouldn't have another dream so significant until I was a young adult. Dreams somehow followed me, guiding my path – leading me away from evil and trying to show me the truth. Most of the time I couldn't even decipher their meanings, but, the hidden theme of this dream was so strong, I couldn't stop until I found its interpretation. Unfortunately, I wouldn't know the interpretation for another thirty years.

This dream pursued me, unchanging, for years. The opening scene is set in the living room of my parents' home. In it, I'm sitting against the back wall, looking toward the foyer. Two single stairs lead out of the foyer into the living room. My bedroom is just above this entryway. Directly over the opening of the stairs is a two-and-a-half-foot portion of wall. This wall became a kind of screen for the dream:

It was nighttime. The moon cast the only light in the dream. The wall above the stairs to the living room now became a viewing window

into my room, but the bedroom was transformed now into an office.
There was a large desk like you'd see in an episode of Perry Mason
but no bed. A blonde was woman standing in front of the desk and my
father was directly behind her. In one harsh, aggressive shove he
pushes her head down flat against the top of the desk and keeps her
pinned there with an unyielding grip on the back of her neck. With
his free hand, he pulls up her skirt and prepares to rape her.

I'd awaken at that exact moment, the dream never playing all the way through, haunting me with its obscurity for years. Nothing was added or appended to the strange black-and-white nightmare. The nightmare always woke me in a panic, a cold dew covering my forehead, and the deadening silence left every limb stricken. For days after the dream, I agonized over the meaning of it and what it might be trying to reveal to me. Or I did as I was taught -- I sometimes tried to bury it, burn it, extinguish the very thought of it. But mostly, the dream left me glossy with an appetite for nothing – its haze hung around as an impending omen.

I've mentioned that my father was my only comfort. In retrospect, clearly, he designed it this way, didn't he? He'd been the very source of my nightmares and he'd also become the only comfort for them. If I could not console myself alone, if the fear gripped too hard, I'd run to his room in the night. This did not happen very often as I needed to fend for myself but at times the terror was too much, and I had to go to him. I had nowhere else to turn. Nightmares and leg pain plagued me most nights as I battled to find rest. It was his power that brought my fear, and it was by his power that the fear could be kept at bay.

When I'd walk into his room in the dead of the night, he'd gently turn on his light, pull my face softly into his bare chest, and hold me for a while. The smell of *Old Spice* floated around him. He'd tell me it was going to be all right. In that moment, it did feel alright. It was one time I could go to him, and he wouldn't get angry at me. The fragrance of his aftershave is now comforting.

His presence soothed my fear, but it did not abate my suffering. As much as I loved being on his bare chest, creating a fantasy that he was a loving father it simply couldn't work.

I was probably five or six when my dad decided that we had too many cats in the world. One of our country cats had just given birth to these beautiful furry babies. My brother and I adored the kittens and were outside playing with them when Dad walked up.

He staged the scene using a large stump for his chopping block and carried a hulking wooden-handled axe. Without a word, Dad reached down, picked up one of the kittens, and placed its head on the rough top of that chopping block. He raised his arm up high and smashed the first little guy in the head using the blunt end of the axe. It slammed so hard into his underdeveloped spongy head that blood immediately gushed from his mouth. His tongue flopped out and his tiny eyes bulged. I couldn't look away. I was paralyzed. It wasn't the first time I'd seen my father kill something.

When we were grown, I asked my brother if he recalled the incident. He said he did. I asked him if he was sure it really happened.

My brother said, "Of course it happened, why?"

I replied, "Because there's just so much bad in my mind, I need to be clear."

Six

D E A T H †

"My silences had not protected me. Your silence will not protect you."
- Audre Lorde

I had stumbled my way into middle school. Most kids don't like these years and neither did I. Often, I came home from school and the house held an audible silence. I enjoyed capturing moments of quiet time when people weren't around. Isolation offered its own form of companionship -- the reliable howling of her rooms, the steadfast tranquility of the night -- but I hated being completely alone in that evil house. Secluded me with my fears and anxieties, my being was racked with non-complicity to the crimes that were hidden there.

With an inability to deny the disturbance I needed a distraction. The loneliness of that house isolated me from anything good. I had no resources but the pain my body played with could be debilitating. To avoid a flood of ideas I could not surrender to, food became a companion. I used my friend often and I knew a bowl of ice cream would do the trick. After piling spoonfuls of frozen treasure into my bowl, I returned to the front room. The window there looked over the field that held the cemetery of the murdered woman. Not remembering details because of the precious work and sting of years of repression, my mind was seeking the truth. Most of the years forgotten memory only returned to me in the form of several aches and pains, but today something different was happening. I kept getting this rugged desire to write on the wall. It was a compulsion that drew me – strange and compelling, it was outside of my mental capacity to decipher. I found a pencil, grabbed a chair, and climbed aboard its unsteady seat. Positioning the pencil on the wall, I began to draw large shaky letters about a foot tall. First, I scratched a D, then forged an E, then continued with the letters A T H.

When the last letter had been written, a new impulse arose in me. I went to the kitchen and grabbed this old knife with a heavy wooden handle. Using the old blade as a nail and Mom's meat cleaver as my hammer, I drove the knife into the wall right after the last letter: an ominous exclamation. I sat and stared at the emblematic graffiti. If no one was going to acknowledge my pain and anguish, I was going to make them see.

My parents would be arriving home soon and I was unsure about how I was going to explain such a crazy thing. I once again found myself covering up the truth (a pattern they taught me!). When they got home, I played the role of a frightened adolescent walking into our empty house and finding the strange inscription. My mom and dad phoned the police. I don't remember having any discussion until the officer's pulled into the driveway and came to the door. Now, I was terrified -- terrified that I'd be in big trouble. The police were taking the report when I spotted the pencil lying where I'd placed it in the planter under the wall. Worried they would somehow find something before I pointed it out, I ran to it, grabbed the pencil, and exclaimed, "Look, here's a pencil."

No one bothered with it. The police took their report and left. Mom and Dad said nothing to me after their departure. My parents would hold the belief to my siblings that I did these crazy things for attention while all along they knew the truth, but the family code of armor was inscribed with denial. Once again, I would take the blame and be my family's scapegoat so they could avoid dealing with the fields of devastation they needed to harvest. You know, there's a funny thing about the attention aspect they so frequently tried to categorize my need with – I never did get any of their attention. Sadly, nothing from the attending officers either.

I didn't know then what drove me to such peculiar behavior. Breaking this all down, it's simple. The wall I chose to use as my canvas upon which I wrote DEATH – that's the same wall used as the screen for my recurring nightmare. The dichotomy of growing up in such abuse is that at the exact time you are burying all abuse through layer upon layer of denial and years of suppression, you are also struggling to remember it all at the same time. Never being talked with about anything of substance as a child, I didn't know how to even explore such craziness.

The gross conclusion I was left with was that I was a fucking mess and no one cared. No one was ever coming into my black hole of need. The embossed heaviness it left with me was staggering but I just had to get on with things. As a child in my parents' home, you didn't ask for anything. Help would be a distant cry that no one would ever hear. I wasn't sure if I was crazy or not, but I was damn scared and needed help. Defending yourself to others about who you are is gut wrenching. The tiring game or worth, suggestion, help. I certainly couldn't see through the veil yet but knew something was behind it. It had nothing to do with creating attention—I wouldn't get it anyway nor did I want it. It had everything to do with returning to the rattling bones just beneath the surface of my mind.

By the time I hit high school, I was a whopping size twenty. Food was everywhere. Readily at my disposal and I had full access. What better way to spend your day but in pleasure? I would eat to the point of exhaustion, take a nap, and after a good rest, I was back at it again. This took my mind to a place of numbness. Filtering through my mind was another savory mixture of food, subsiding my subliminal messages. Sometimes I didn't stop until my belly threw out all that had been stuffed into it but I was good with that. It was a far cry from the anguish I was carrying. I can't tell you what the food tasted like; it wasn't about that. It was a mindless activity that helped me thrive on something other than my anxiety, pain, and emptiness. A great distraction. Addiction, many would scream. But food saved me. It saved me from a complete life of despair. I would've endlessly suffered through the day contemplating ways to self-destruct. By that, I mean suicide. There was no other way out. I hadn't gained the autonomy of adulthood and I was stuck. Utterly hopeless. Anything that made my flesh feel better, I honor now. It was a breath of fresh air to me. Anything but the misery of this bleak existence.

Needing something in a tangible way to sooth me, I reached for anything. Made to gorge on my parents' destruction, now I had some kind of choice.

I made it out. That was what mattered.

I have found greater ways to love myself, but still will honor those days when I could bring comfort into an abyss where there was none. Anything that paused the pain was a friend. I understand that now.

As I ate my way through the years, the consequence of those extra calories caught up with me. I stopped looking in the mirror when I couldn't find clothes big enough to wear. Disguising my pain through hidden food binges brought out by the family ridicule. They loved to shame, and I was now a perfect target. My brother made relentless jokes about my weight and my mother and father went into their full-blown control about how to fix it.

My father bought me a book called *Help Lord, the Devil Wants Me Fat*. I read the book in one night. It directed me to fast for ten days to break the spell food held over my life. I think I almost died (not really, but it was grueling) and I didn't make the entire ten-day fast.

A scriptural approach to a trim and attractive body. As Lovett puts it, the devil has "unleashed an army of glutton demons on American Christians." Lovett calls food, "The most subtle way the devil gets us to defile our bodies," and writes, "We head for the cupboard or refrigerator without realizing that we're OBEYING THE DEVIL. From his stronghold he sits back and beams." Wait, what? This was what my father gave to me in the name of Jesus? I was thirteen. Did I even want a trim and attractive body, yet? Fuck no. I wanted love. I needed a book to cure my miserable pain. Can you blame Satan? Sure, especially when he lives inside your home.

I think the Spirit of Religion created this ugly book. This is classic grooming for an incestuous father. He didn't want to rape a fat girl!

I was now being ridiculed by my entire family. My father brings in the devil – always this common thread my father used. The devil made me do it and now the devil was making me do this. How can a house stand with the devil and now attempt to call him out as the culprit? A house divided cannot stand, right?

My mother's great attempt to help me better my appearance was on the advent of Easter. All the other kids got a beautiful array of chocolates and goodies. I was given a basket of sugar-free hard candies that tasted like unlined paper. On top of these atrocious candies was a fuzzy blue rabbit that you could wind up and it played a tune. Seriously? I was thirteen and this was the first thing you ever gave me, Mom? My mother called the rabbit, the *Habit Rabbit*. She stood right beside my father in this new grooming ploy to get me skinny. I wanted to tell her to take that rabbit and shove it up her ass. You see, I had failed again. I was fat. She wasn't. I showed my pain. She didn't. And my appearance was not acceptable to them.

Neither of my parents' gifts worked for me. What worked was the green Schwinn bike I got. I rode that two-wheeled friend all over the roads of Livingston Mountain. We had a German Shepherd named Buck and he ran alongside me. I lost sixty pounds in the summer of my sophomore year. Oh, and I scarcely ate. One meal a day – like a can of spinach and a few Saltines. Before school started, I went to the local mall and walked into a jeans' store that all the other kids had jeans from. The clerk asked what size she could get me, but I had no idea. She laughed and thought I was joking. I left my sophomore year at size twenty and returned my junior year a junior size nine. This would open for me the world of boys and a different kind of addiction. I also could dress like my peers. What a difference that made. The appearance of fitting in. This new body was not going to be just for my father's pleasure. I was going to use it to get the hell out of his house.

Growing into adolescence, I yearned to explore the opposite sex, but Dad was reluctant to let me be free. I was guarded closely by his watch. Getting my license was like receiving a pardon from the warden. I could get in a car and drive away – even if just for a few hours. I was alone, away from that house. No one could monitor my every move. Oh, my father wouldn't stop trying, he'd just have to look harder for it. As a matter of fact, I did push the envelope and Dad responded in measure.

One night, I was to attend a teen bible study. Intending to head that way, I decided at the last minute to go to a boy's house. I would never have been allowed a boyfriend, so I'd have to sneak in time with him. Of course, this boy was much older than I was. I was sixteen and he was twenty-one. He had his own place, where we drank whiskey and listened to music. I could finally be the kind of adult I'd watched as a child. I liked it.

I left his house and drove away, liking him but liking the feeling of choice more. In the driveway my father met me at the side of the car with his open-handed slams into my face and head. His constant barrage of hits continued onto the porch, through the doorway, and into the entry. I was falling up the stairs from his backhanding reproachful hits, when my mother finally intervened and told him to stop hitting me.

He demanded to know where I'd been. I told him bible study. He told me he'd received a phone call that the study was cancelled. It was as if my father shared a pervading omniscience with the Almighty. He had a way of always being in the know. I couldn't hide anything from him but my ability to not need his love. That was my secret. A profound secret that would guard my heart from any love for years. As I was taught, no love in, no love out.

The next day, I came home from school to a dozen red roses in my room. Just like a lover would give you after a fight. The card read, "I'm sorry for the pain I put in your heart last night, Dad." He wasn't sorry, but scared he was losing his grip on me and feared his forceful brutality would push me away.

He was right. His flowers didn't help. They made me sick to my stomach. His sick foolish way of treating me paved a path for many of the men that would pick me later in life. Did my father know that he was betrothing me to such a burden? Did he care? I'm okay that he didn't love me, but couldn't he have at least explained to me what I should being look for in a man? Couldn't he have shared his experiences with bad people and how I should avoid them?

Oh, that's right, he was bad, and I think not able or willing to look for anything good. How then could he ever share anything of value with me. Hope deferred does indeed make the heart sick.

He and Mom went out of town for a weekend shortly after this time. He was away! I had a car and a license and a sense of freedom. I went back to that boy's house, but this time he poured us both a Black Velvet and coke and turned on the music. After a few of those, he walked me back to his room. I didn't want to have any kind of sexual activity, but what I did want was the power to choose. I chose to give myself to him. I hated it. It made me feel powerless. I lay there with my mind racing the word S T O P. I hadn't chosen anything but to show up at his house. After I made the choice to go with a man, he could do whatever he wanted. I had never been taught how to say no, how to own my own body and have boundaries. I felt terrible about myself, and it threw me back into the feeling of being abused but I liked being with him. Someone finally saw me. Another dichotomy.

That night, I drove back to my parents' house and my brother was waiting for me. Furious over my time with another man, he explained he was in charge. Perplexed that he exercised ownership of me now, too, I just walked away.

Through the years my brother always wanted to chat about what "We did together." He wanted to know if I remembered. I did not – until I did.

The men in the family seemed to single me out. Maybe I just did not see their other targets.

Only once did I run away to my girlfriend's house for a few days. We played records and smoked cigarettes. I loved it. Her mom gave her a lot of freedom and I'd never known what that felt like. I wanted to stay, but my wings were clipped, and I hadn't earned them yet. I still had a term to serve under my father's regime.

As I knew he would, Dad showed up outside their house and sat there. I saw his car from the window and my heart sank. I told my girlfriend I had to go. She begged me to stay, but she had no idea the unthinkable battle that would ensue if I did. I didn't have the strength, nor did I have the words to explain my entanglement. I was underage, did not have authority over my own life yet, and no formed language of explanation to ask for help.

I opened the front door and dolefully walked to my father's car. A strange current in my veins said he loved me, but I knew better. I'd have to find another way out of his camp.

I was left with so many questions as I moved into young adulthood. At first, walking away from him meant the bomb threats of his temper would be ending. That was a good thing. I could begin to search for the landmines of his manipulations he'd built into me, but I'd need help getting away from him. That I knew. I was still left to walk with the age-old question: what was this war between me and my parents even for?

My father, like most abusers, was very good at getting me back under his spell. Any time I felt like not wanting him, not feeling love for him, or despising his lack of attention (another dichotomy), he would call and set up a watch party for a movie he had selected. He would set the stage for the movie in such a way that you couldn't wait to see it. Then, the ritual of our fantastic popcorn.

We also played board games. *Risk* was one of his favorite games. *Risk* is a strategy board game of conflict and conquest where players may form and dissolve alliances during the game. The goal is to occupy every territory on the board and in doing so, eliminate the other players. With a roll of the dice, you battle for territory. The winner is the person holding the most land at the end of the game.

I wanted to learn how to win this game in real life and kick my father's ass.

Seven

Phantom Pain

"The problem is that we always look for the missing piece
of the puzzle instead of finding a place for the one in our
hand."
- Alina Radoi

I got my license the day I turned sixteen. That plastic pass gave me freedom to get into a car, start it, and drive off that mountain, even just for a few hours at a time. Wow! It was the best feeling I had ever had in my small, bruised world. Cruising the gut – a coined term from my area. It was an activity enjoyed by local teenagers where I lived in the '80s. We'd load our cars with friends and drive slowly along the main downtown shopping street on weekend summer nights.

At the local Dairy Queen, we'd make our turn and cruise down Main Street making the forever circle by turning and going back up Broadway. Inside car after car, was boy after boy. I felt new freedom with each smile I delivered.

I started drinking around this time. I loved it. It stopped my confusion, stopped my anxiety – it damn near seemed to stop every bad feeling I had. I didn't have to think about anything when I drank, and the boys seemed to like my new slimmer figure, youthful beauty, and a tender, conforming personality (I'd been taught to be a doormat).

Of course, I was pretty good at understanding what a man wanted – Dad and my brother taught me well.

I dated a little bit and then ran into a boy named Richard one night. He was a rebel without a cause and an intimidating 6'4" stature. He would fight anyone without reason and was filled with rage. You did not want to get in this man's way. He'd defy and betray anything, and he didn't need an alibi because he saw nothing wrong with getting his hands dirty. In fact, he seemed to enjoy it. Plus, he picked me. He saw my abused soul and knew he could do anything to me. I understood this kind of control and in many ways felt I needed it. I viewed his unrestrained force as a kind of strength, a strength I didn't possess.

One day after school Richard was waiting for me. I stayed late for an afterschool event, so it wasn't the usual time I left. How did he know I'd be walking out at this odd hour? The familiarity drew me to him. He seemed to have a similar omnipresence about him to what my father possessed. Were these two men in cohorts? Did their legions belong together fortified somehow against me.

I got into the car with him, and he drove to a local drive-in burger joint. He ordered a burger, fries, and coke but didn't ask me if I wanted anything (a pattern he never stopped even with his own children). Then, we drove to the river. I knew I didn't matter to him. I didn't much like the way he looked, and his demeanor was mean and controlling. Today I would have told him to move on down the road.

I had never been late getting home from school before and the conversation was a blur because I was panicking about the prospect of my father waiting for me. I was embarrassed to tell Richard I needed to get home. It wouldn't have mattered anyway. He took his time and then drove me up the mountain to my father's house.

I was two hours late.

The car had not stopped before my father's clinched hands and piercing rage flew at the car. He firmly told me to get into the house. Richard got out of the car and stood in front of my dad. I couldn't hear what Dad was bellowing at him, but his tone said he was telling him he was not welcome and not to come back.

Peering from the window, I could see that Richard held no respect (nor any fear) for this father figure screeching at him. I loved that.

As my father read Richard his riot act, I was sure this would be the end of ever seeing him again. But Richard drove to the nearest store and called me right away. He asked, "Are you okay?"

Besides my grandmother, that was the very first time anybody had asked me if I was okay. It was a turning point, helping me gain freedom from my parents. He was going to be my help.

Sensing the dark control in him and wanting my own space, I tried to break up with him -- that didn't go well. He drove me about twenty miles from my parents' home and demanded that I not break up with him. When I told him I hadn't changed my mind, he stopped the car and told me to walk home. This was in an era before cell phones, and we were in a remote area. I conceded and stayed with him from that day forward. We were married a few months later as I knew I wasn't going to get him to leave me alone.

It probably didn't matter who I married, I simply needed to be free from my father's house. I had entertained thoughts of suicide. I fantasized about what it would feel like to get my car up to about eighty miles an hour and just smash full speed into a cement wall. What would the twisted metal smell like? The impact would take all the pressure from me. Suicide would stay with me as a hidden theme, one no one would notice but I kept it as my friend. A fantasy of a way out someday.

Before we married, Richard took me on a romantic rendezvous. I was seventeen years old. At a shabby motel on 82nd Avenue, he registered, and returned with the keys to a room. We then went to a Mexican diner, and I was excited, but something was wrong. Internally, I was freaking out, but I never tipped my hand that panic was rushing through me.

We left and stopped at a small market for bubble bath and champagne. I knew we'd be going back to the motel room and couldn't figure out what the heck was wrong with me. My legs had begun that old, dull ache since we first pulled into the motel. We arrived back and parked.

My legs were in such intense pain I couldn't walk. They'd become useless, immobilized with fear. What was my body doing to me?

I was terribly embarrassed. Why now? Was I scared of sex? I knew what was about to happen. I couldn't find the answer in my mind that night in 1982 but again my body was screaming at me.

Richard had to carry me up the stairs to the room and he sat me down on the bed. I asked him to run a hot bath and put me in it. That would get my legs to stop aching and work properly as I had done many times through my childhood, and it did. It jogged my memory that something had taken place in a motel room with Dad and Craig. That came to me, but I could not recall what happened.

By now, the jets in the bathtub had propelled bubbles about an inch thick across the bathroom floor and we began laughing. I was so relieved that he didn't ask me more about what happened and why I couldn't walk. I clearly did not know why my body shut down but was by now used to the incomprehensible pain it often produced. I just wanted to fucking live, so I drank the champagne and got into the bath. I did not want to bring my parents' disgusting choices with me.

The champagne I'd guzzled helped and we moved on with our night. The experience bonded me to him. He was the first person in my life who sat next to my pain. I couldn't keep it hidden and he hadn't rejected me for it but had shown kindness and understanding.

We married soon thereafter in 1982. The night before the wedding, Richard and his buddies threw a bachelor party in our apartment. When I returned to the apartment the day after our wedding, I found a blue dress that some women had left. Richard had surely been unfaithful that night.

After two months, I too cheated. I went out with my girlfriend to a local dance club. I was only eighteen and this freedom, I loved it. I also loved to dance and the warm attention of men. The more I drank, the more I danced. Before I knew it, I was leaving with a man. I wasn't the best at boundaries with men, so the slightest nudge from them earned the response sought. My upbringing had taught me well: I complied. The problem was I had a contract to another man.

The next morning when I awoke and had to return to my husband, reality hit. I didn't like the feeling of betraying another human. I didn't like having to lie to cover up that betrayal. That next day, I told myself I would not be living this pattern. It didn't feel good. I decided to tell my husband what I had done. He made me pay for my confession, but I never cheated on him again for the next seventeen years.

After that, infidelity seemed to be instinctive in my ex and he used my mistake as a license to do as he pleased. I know now that he would have done that anyway. Of course, because I had been *bad and cheated*, I felt I deserved his abusive treatment. I was not old enough to go to bars with him, so he often left me at home. These were very dark times. I wanted his love and protection and yet received only rejection most of the time. This heightened my feelings of being unworthy. Instead of walking away at this early stage, it depleted any strength I may have had – which wasn't much.

He broke me more. He was a brutish man who held no loyalty. He used his intimidating stature on everyone – grocery clerks included. You did not get in this man's way. If you did, he would move you. He cheated, he drank obsessively, and he followed no one's rules but his own. You couldn't leave him. If you tried, you'd be hurt. I understood this game well, so I stayed. At least I wasn't with my parents anymore.

I've been asked through the years, as many abused women are, why did I stay seventeen years? That isn't a difficult question to answer. We met as most teenagers do, out driving our local streets. He told me history about his own abusive upbringing, and I was thrown into the role I had known so well – fix it for him and he was going to fix me, too.

He also had a loving side to him. One night, before we married, we were lying on his bed, in each other's arms, the radio played softly in the background -- a song by Seafood Momma (who later changed their name to Quarter Flash) came on: "I'm Gonna' Harden My Heart and Swallow My Tears." He told me that every time he heard that song, he thought of me. Again, he saw my pain – or at least I believed he did. I had so little in life that any kind of acknowledgment felt momentous.

Not long after I married, unburdened from my father's watchful control, odd things happened. When we'd make love, tears would stream down my face – tears I couldn't stop. I would just turn my face to the side and wait for the act to be over. Richard accepted it. He may have used it against me, but I didn't see it that way then.

In 1985, our first child was born. A beautiful, brown-skinned baby girl. We named her Brittany Lynne. She ignited in me a love I had never known. I cherished her and it gave me a reason to live. Brooke Ashley came along in 1988. She was a creature of beauty with a delightful disposition. My heart was full.

It was after Brooke's birth that a first real memory of abuse came to me. Brittany would have been close to three years old. The time my abuse likely began.

During a visit to my in-laws', my mother-in-law and I took her ten-year-old daughter out to get some pumpkin ice cream for everyone. We went to one Dairy Queen and then another – we couldn't find the pumpkin flavor we sought. Then, I remembered about this off-the-beaten-track Dairy Queen that was in my old childhood suburb. We took the main street, a street that would have taken us right to it, but we encountered an odd detour. This diversion led us directly past the house I lived in until I was four. I hadn't been by since we'd moved out of it in 1968 or, if so, I didn't remember.

As we approached the house, I asked Debbie to slow down for a minute because, wow –there it was. That house! The drapes on the front window happened to be open. I could see into the small living room -- it had seemed so big when I lived there. In my mind's eye, I saw the one-quarter-sized pink couch that used to be there. An image of my father appeared in front of me, on his knees, preparing to rape me. This was the first rape memory for me, but many would come. I began to cry almost before the car came to a full stop.

Then my sister-in-law, who was only ten said, "Jodie, are you okay?"

Her words shot me right back to the need to close that memory down, post haste – for the sake of those around me. My pelvis area began to ache before we even reached Dairy Queen, which was only about four blocks away. Another layer of the onion of denial was being peeled away.

I wasn't prepared for this kind of visceral physical memory. By the time we got back to Debbie's house, I couldn't stand up straight. It was horribly frustrating to have this feeling overtake me, but I couldn't shut it off. I walked up to Richard and told him we had to leave. I never asked for what I needed, ever, so he listened to me, and we left.

We got home, I put the kids to bed, and rushed to take a hot bath. Tears swollen with grief of years past steadily flowed. Tantalized with my new life with my children, these memories threatened to bring that to an end. It was the onslaught of the pending tidal wave. I had little power over the process or when the memories stopped. I turned the water off and the phone rang.

My middle sister, Crissy, asked, "Are you okay?"

I asked why she called because it was late at night.

She said, "I just felt like something was wrong with you."

And, indeed, there was something wrong with me.

Not long after, I took this memory of being raped to my mother. She had asked me in the past if there was ever a time I screamed, "Dad, stop."

Her questioning an obvious way to remove herself from accountability.

My brother lived in Hawaii, and we asked him if he could come home so we could talk about family issues of the past. Immediately, he said he knew what this was about: Dad and sexual stuff. He had reminded me through the years that there was something deeply imbedded in us that was not right. He flew home.

We convened the meeting at Crissy's house with all four siblings and Mom. Sharing details of my journey by our old house sparked stories from them.

My brother shared about Dad's blue truck. He told of being small enough to stand next to dad in the truck. He recalled spitting out semen after being made to perform oral sex on our father. He then told of going on fishing trips with Dad and Craig. He told us they filmed him going to the bathroom. He told us that sometimes he could still smell Craig.

My oldest sister remembered Dad behind her and rubbing himself on her. She didn't know if it was more, but it was worrisome. A few days later she would tell me more.

My middle sister shared nothing at that time.

We decided as a family we would go to my father and confront him.

We pulled up to his house with so much fear, even as a unit, that we backed the car into the driveway so we could escape quickly if things went haywire.

We walked into Dad's jaw clenched with defiance and a noticeable tick in his check. His demeanor, dank with anger -- hands in a lose fist on his knees. He said nothing as we all found a place to sit.

I sat directly in front of my father. It still made me sad seeing him sit there. He was always truly alone while on this planet. It may have been the pain that twisted his soul. Codependent themes were surely present in me.

My sisters sat behind us, my mother beside us, and my brother found a spot in the farthest corner away from this arena. He cocked his chair, so his body wasn't facing any of us.

Fear dominated this house still.

I opened with, "Dad, you took my virginity."

He said nothing.

Our conversation continued one-sided as I shared stories of abuse – somehow becoming the voice of confrontation for all of us kids.

My father spoke "Claude, what do you remember?"

My brother shared a time when the two of them stopped by a lady's house down the street. They pulled into her driveway and chatted for a while. He wondered who she was and why they were there.

I understood why that was the only story he had the strength to tell.

When that story was shared, my mother flew out of her chair and rushed at my father. She was screaming at him, believing the story my brother shared was an act of adultery. All of us intervened because a fight ensued. She took her shoe off and tried to reach through us to clobber him with it.

The meeting abruptly ended with that dramatic but laughable act.

She was not upset about the child abuse.

After pulling our mother away from Dad, we all ran to our getaway car and sped off his property as fast as we could.

The ensuing days, months, and years were not good. My mother left my dad and moved in with me and my family. My girls were very young. The morning after she arrived, she called out that I needed to come to her quickly. She said she could not move. She said it was her back and I needed to get the bible and read aloud to her. She explained to me how she woke up in the middle of the night and Dad was over her talking in tongues. This was ghostly. I had children in the house with her. She felt he had cursed her through his words and that was the reason she was not able to move. I told her I would massage her back to help.

Her back was miserably bruised. If this was a spiritual war, she would lose. The bruises on her back looked like she had been beaten. I asked her to tell me the truth -- did Dad do this to you?

She told me he had not hit her but that it was a spiritual attack from his words. Terrified, I opened the bible and read aloud to her. Within an hour or so she was able to move and get herself out of bed. Such evil I was raised in. It wasn't a battle I wanted to look at often, but it was a battle I found myself in again and again.

A few days later, my oldest sister called me to ask how Mom was doing. She had been the caretaker to us kids while mom worked. Her dark hair was thick and brittle – almost an indication of the decay placed in her soul. She then told me she remembered a time when she walked in, and Dad was abusing me. She described him in front of me on his knees. I was lying on my back on the small, pie-shaped pink couch we had on Delaware Lane. I told her I remembered. She assured me that she did not know how to help. I could feel the anguish in her heart for her lack of protection over me. It was not her fault and yet she struggled, being the oldest – she felt she had some ownership in this all. I do not hold her responsible for his sins or my mother's.

Eager to have my father confess, I called him. He answered the phone and didn't hang up. That was a good sign. Sharing more detail with him, I told him I grew up with a dreadful vaginal odor as a kid. The odor so offending my brother made fun of me for it. As an adult, the doctor told me I carried chlamydia. I shared with him that mom dealt with chlamydia too for years.

I asked him, "Do you realize you gave it to me, too?"

His response was staggering "You know, baby girl, Satan planted that in you as a child to destroy me today."

I was in obvious despair. I didn't drink much in those days at all, my children were little and I lived close to the religion I was brought up in, but this night, I did. Richard went out often, and this time, I joined him. We went to a bar with live music and before we left, I took a few shots of tequila to quell the enormous pain. We sat at a table with friends and across the room, I noticed Richard's sister. I'd built what I thought was a good friendship with my sister-in-law. She was a pretty lady, and I appreciated her attitude toward life -- effortless in the way she seemed to take what she wanted from men and from the world.

Richard went over and said hi, but she didn't return the welcoming wave to me. Something had happened between us, but I wasn't sure what. I didn't really care at this point -- it was trivial in comparison to the chaos boiling in my soul. I walked to the bathroom.

My sister-in-law happened to be in the stall beside me. I said, "Hi."

No reply.

Her friend asked who I was.

She replied, "That's my brother's wife. Let's just get out of here."

Her rejecting words made my anger boil. I was going to confront her unfeeling words.

I still don't know how I got off that toilet, zipped up my pants, and caught her before she walked out of that small bathroom door. I stopped her and asked what her statement meant.

She looked at me and said, "I don't know what you're talking about."

Her words, coupled with the confusion and rejection of my last few days, shot me directly into a wave of anger I'd never encountered. She turned to walk out of the bathroom to leave me behind in shame.

I followed her. Grabbing her arm, I spun her around toward me. A nearby bouncer walked over to ask if there was a problem. The last thing I remember was putting my hands behind my back and telling him, "Nope, there's no problem." Then, I blacked out. I'd never done that before. The next thing I remember is being on top of my sister-in-law, choking her. Someone tried to pull me off her. They got me off and I ran to try to get at her again.

When I woke up the next morning, I said to Richard, "Oh, I don't think I want to wake up."

I remembered the fight but didn't know how it started. "What happened last night?"

Richard told me that he was in the lounge and heard there was a catfight in the foyer. He ran out to watch and saw that it was his sister and wife on the floor. He was the one who pulled me off her. I couldn't take the betrayal from her. I needed her friendship, and for whatever reason, she wasn't willing to be there for me. I didn't drink again for years. I'd always been a very quiet, nonaggressive person and this version of myself unsettled me.

I began a journal of the memories that would come back to me after that time. I have the writings from 1990−91. The entries were all focused on the sexual abuse that occurred, but nothing about the murder, yet. Now in my twenties, I wrote some about the effect my mother left on me. I wrote:

I felt a strong protection for my mother. She, too, was being victimized. She was being emotionally starved while at the same time forced to gorge on mental anguish. I would have to help, thus perpetuating the misguided role of heroine.

Wow, hadn't her message been left with me? It was my job to care for her. Not only did I have to care for my dad's wellbeing and happiness, but my mother also asked the same from me. It continued to say:

> If the courage within me ever rose to discuss this hidden evil, I would never betray my loyalty to her happiness. One more blow and she might not stand. Without her, my world would be a bleak existence of shame. I must prove to her that I am content. At all costs, we must keep our family together. We need each other. If one person is missing, we will all explode.

I eventually did walk away from this role, but it was no easy task. It ripped at the connective tissue of who my parents had raised me to be. Deeper still, it ripped at the fantasy of who I wanted them to be. Specifically, who I fantasized my mother would be.

Her sexual abuse of me was the last memory I uncovered. It was the hardest to find because she was all I had left of the story. I wanted to create a story that included a mother who cared for her youngest daughter -- me. A mother who intensely protected me – no matter the cost of appearances or her marriage. Not a mother who aligned herself closer to my father by abusing me.

It took much of my life to forge the path to this story. My mother's abuse was a major part of what I wanted to keep hidden. It was the last and most heinous piece of it all. It was harder than the murder because it left me completely alone. It was the deepest attack. She was the last effort I had to pretend I came from love.

I have endured too much abuse at the hands of others because of my dissociative behaviors. "Dissociation means simultaneously knowing and not knowing." That's from the book, The Body Keeps the Score. It goes on to say, "When you don't feel real nothing matters, which makes it impossible to protect yourself from danger." *Body Keeps the Score*, Van Der Kolk, M.D., Page 121.

On full autopilot, I had become disabled by my ability to smile and live in death. My soul had been invaded and overtaken by factors that I could not cope with. So, the beautiful gift of dissociation, again, became my best friend.

The problem with that friendship was that it enabled me to stay in such abusive situations that other people would have run screaming from. The dissociation led me to see the abuse, while at the very same time, I did not see it at all.

This is such an elusive dichotomy.

The abuse infringed on everything good in me and on my children's lives, but I denied the power and effect of that abuse in the same breath. This torture lives in a realm all its own.

It is a terrible flight pattern.

When my fog was lifted and I could see, the heaviness left was tremendously painful. The destructive forces I grew up around brought little comfort to the isolated land of destruction I once again found myself in. The suffering it injected into my children's lives was a very hard pill to swallow. I forgive myself but I sometimes want to hold myself in contempt for the damage I caused by not putting this miserable puzzle together fast enough.

I had become disabled by the great ability to deny. Isn't that what dissociative patterns are all about? A coat with a thick lining of impenetrable denial.

The life I found myself in at this time felt different. I had a husband and two children. I was going to build what I didn't have – at all costs -- but this destructive connection I had to my family of origin continued to cloud my way. It guided my days, and I was driven by some primal force to move closer to them. It saddens me how much time with my children was spent on my pursuit to correct – or hell, merely learn -- what was in my past. They didn't have all of me, that's for sure. Neither did their father.

As time went by, my marriage continued to decay. The kids' dad had also grown up in an abusive, neglectful family, so it wasn't surprising that the two of us came together. The more he raged, the more I tried to comply. The more he cheated, the more I tried to look better, cook better, and perform better.

The never-ending cycle.

Eight

Prophecy

"I am no bird; and no net ensnares me."
– Charlotte Brontë

As my family of origin struggled to move past our disclosures of abuse, my father fell ill. He, of course, maintained that we were all liars and had no idea what we were talking about. By this time my mother had moved back in with him, after a short stint of living on her own. She said, "I was lonely. None of you kids ever came to see me."

I can't image why.

Dad was put in the hospital. My mother was stricken with a fear that she may lose him. She was a blubbering mess, clutching her purse as if holding onto my father's soul. She could not lose him, that was clear. She had us go to the hospital chapel and pray for him. She wouldn't hold up well without his dark strength. Who would she fight with? Who would she love? Who would protect her hidden evil?

Eventually, the doctor came out and informed my mother about a procedure he was planning to run, and she literally collapsed to the floor. In truth, it made me sick. I hated watching how much she loved this sick, miserable man. I was still close to my siblings at this time and told everyone I would keep watch through the night on Dad's condition, that they needed to take Mom home. They did and I stayed and prayed for him until morning.

I was terrified to stay at the hospital. I didn't want to sit next to my father alone but had been given that role a long time before. Growing up, my father had pitted us against each other and the special attention he'd given me angered the entire household. Hadn't they seen the price I paid?

My father was in ICU. I needed someone with me to wrap my panicked nerves. I called my mother-in-law, Deb, and she came to the hospital and sat with me until morning.

In the coming days, as he recovered, I continued to visit him. One day after he was moved from the ICU, I came to see him and sat down beside his bed. I looked at the breathing tube down his throat and took his hand in mine and caressed it. I was betrothed to him, and he knew it. His restrained eyes looked at me in defeat. Not being able to speak, a very small tear rolled out of his eye and down his temple. I wanted to believe with all my heart that Dad would recover and say he was terribly sorry, that he loved us all, and it was going to be okay. His inability to speak enabled me to project my deepest longings onto him and to briefly fantasize about his impending apology to the family, to me.

When the tube was finally removed a few days later, I walked into his hospital room, anticipating comforting words of affirmation about the pain inflicted by his hands. I sat gently on the bed, and he pulled me close to him in an embrace.

He whispered in my ear, "I've got my life, I've got my baby girl, but I've still got this lie."

My heart fell to the floor. My dreams of him loving us were smashed. I pushed him away from me, stood, and walked out of that room.

I only saw my father a handful of times after that. He had chosen deceit and the battle between us was on.

About six months before this illness, I'd dreamt that my father was milling about his house. The dream began with a man crawling in a downstairs window at my dad's house. He stayed in the house a long time. The dream finished with my father walking away from the house with a limp. It was strange to me at the time but also something I couldn't ignore.

I prayed about the dream. I knew that the man who crawled through my dad's window was evil. It was like death had come in. I opened my bible and ironically read about a six-month period. Strange to me, but notable, I looked ahead at the calendar six months and made note of it. Almost to the day six months later, my father entered the hospital – fighting for his life.

When Dad returned home from the hospital – yep, he walked with a limp.

Was this odd dream a prophecy fulfilled?

I was in a true battle of good and evil. Just like they depict in a comic-book story. Who could stand the strongest for their side? I had heard about spiritual warfare but through these strange dreams, I was being taught.

I had another significant dream in my early twenties that began to unravel his cold love for me. In this dream, my father was holding an exaggeratedly large syringe. With Dad being a diabetic, I was used to seeing syringes, but not of this size. On the side, in very large writing, were the words: "LOVE SERUM."

Dad took my forearm. He brought the syringe close, with the needle's plunger up and ready to deliver.

I awoke in dread and confusion. The dream was with me that next morning and I tried to explore its meaning. Clearly this contrived love between my father and me was not right. This was not the natural love a child holds for a parent. His gripping control enveloped every bond we shared.

That same day, I walked to my mailbox and opened its door to discover a letter inside. It was from my father.

After my marriage, he and I had been somewhat estranged. This letter was the first Dad had ever written to me. I opened it up and found cash tucked between the pages. I put the money aside and started to read. It was a love letter. His words beckoned my return to him, to our love. He reminded me how much I meant to him, how life without me wouldn't be as good. Then, he wrote, "I've done nothing to harm you." The background music underlying his words of love ended, abruptly. The warning of the dream I had had the very night before shouted at me not to listen to his words. The dream tried to persuade me, even before the arrival of the letter, that this love serum my father built me for would ultimately take my life if I accepted it.

I chose then that I would not take this fake love into my heart any longer. To heal, I would need to stay away from it.

It's not an easy task to walk away from a token of love. A child's deepest longing is to be loved by her parent. Caressed and kissed with hands that bring peace not brutality.

The two twenty-dollar bills would be an inward bound prescription that could cause me to stay in denial if I kept it. I knew this because he used the same ploy throughout my childhood. At Christmas, I would receive an extra present --a gift my brothers and sisters despised me for -- but one that I loved because it meant Daddy saw me. His manipulations were tactics to smooth over past harm and groom me for future abuse.

On that realization I took the money into my bathroom, shut the door so my children wouldn't see, and lit those twenties on fire and threw them into the toilet.

I could have used that money. I was a stay-at-home mom and we had only one income. It felt strange as I torched those bills in secrecy, but I needed my freedom from him more. Leaving my parents' house did nothing to stop my pain.

I had become a prisoner by crimes I didn't commit.

Nine

Trains, Planes & Automobiles

"Let yourself be gutted. Let it open you. Start there."
– Cheryl Strayed from Tiny Beautiful Things

My brother had moved to Hawaii to run from illicit-drug complications at home and began working for Hawaiian air. Richard was a brick mason and belonged to an international union that had an office on Oahu. We decided to move our family to Hawaii and rent a place with my brother. After a very short year, we returned to the mainland and moved into a small town in Washington.

My oldest daughter, Brit, was in kindergarten and my little one, Brooke, was just three. I was a stay-at-home home in those days – the best job I've ever had. My girls were opposite in nature but close. Their thick dark blonde hair, beautiful skin, and striking eyes showed sisterhood.

One night, we had a party at a friend's house and Richard left to run to the store. The girls and I went home because he still hadn't returned by nightfall. About 4 or 5am, he came home.

The next day, I received a call from an angry husband, screaming on the phone, "Your husband did coke with my wife last night. I need to talk to him – now!"

Richard took the phone from my ear and hung up. I was devastated. I was just like my mom in the sense that this was now my family. He was my husband. I didn't want to share him. I wanted him to be devoted to our family. But this was my normal by now, still too broken to leave.

I tried to write whenever I could. When Brooke was a baby, I had a vision of this book. On the cover was a woman wearing a prison-issued dress sitting on a concrete floor. One window cast a shadow onto her downtrodden appearance. The title of the book was, *A Prisoner by No Crime of My Own.*

I wasn't allowed friends and found maintaining relationships outside of my narcissistic husband was a daunting task. His control was quite happy to have his wife and kids home waiting for him. Away from the world, away from everything. I had enough to try to keep afloat but could've really used a good friend during those years. My dad and I remained distant. I don't remember my mom much at all during these years. We were never close, but my father! I struggled with my choices to stay away from him. I missed him and yet, was very scared of him. My brother and I spoke often during this time. He was trying to change a lifestyle he found himself in and we tried to be there for each other. The same was true of my middle sister. The three of us struggled to find our way and hold on to what love we tried to hide away for each other.

My brother was living in California by now and was home visiting. During all this family turmoil, my sister told us that she believed her son was being abused by his father. She had very explicit examples of what she'd seen. The three of us panicked. We had to do something to get him safe. Fear was immense in our lives. We didn't realize we had options and that our voices could give us strength. The only choice we saw was to run, and run we did. It was Christmastime and the presents were wrapped under the tree. We plotted our escape. My brother was single, so his escape was easy. I was married with two kids. My sister was also married with three sons.

We made a plan. In retrospect, it was a lousy plan, but nonetheless, we tried what we knew to do at the time to keep my nephew safe. We were going to load up in the middle of the night while our husbands were at work and drive to my brother's house in California. We'd figure out from there what to do next. We wrapped fake Christmas gifts to put under the tree and packed up the real gifts so the kids would have something on our journey. As planned, we woke the kids and told them we were going to Disneyland and off we went. Five kids, three adults, one Chevy Trail Blazer, and all the stuff we could take, including pancake syrup -- I think my sister's attempt at bringing some normalcy with us.

By the time we reached California, the three of us had discussed that our husbands would soon be on our trail. They were both crazed men when it came to anybody trying to leave them. In fear, we changed our course, ditched the car, and jumped on a train with the kids. Destination unknown.

The only place in those days to find help, we somehow surmised, was to go to Oprah. Crazy, but she was the only person who was listening to and actively helping abuse victims. This whacked religion that we came from offered no source of help. The cops were not a reliable source of protection. When I wrote "D E A T H" on my parents' wall and they called the police, I had this secret hope someone would notice. They did not. My father called the police when a trespasser appeared on his property. The cops responded and removed the trespasser. When my sister was hit by her husband, the cops were called, and no one was removed from any property. In those days (and maybe even now) the police didn't do a lot to help abuse victims.

So, we went naively believing Oprah would listen. We got off the train, rented a car, and drove across the country. Later, we would refer to the trip as *'planes, trains and automobiles.'*

We finally made it to Chicago at Christmas. We had our babies with us and needed to create a holiday, so we headed out to find a tree.

The lots were all closed. We drove around looking with no luck. I had an idea -- we could gather the riffraff limbs that were lying around on these closed tree lots and make a tiny Christmas tree of our own. We brought those boughs to our meager hotel room. I filled the ice bucket and placed the boughs in, standing up. Now, decorations. I used tissue to create a flower-bow effect. Finally, our tree was complete.

The next day, we eagerly went to Harpo productions, home of the Oprah show, but they were closed for the holiday season – two long weeks. Our hearts sank. The kids were safe, but what were we to do next? It makes me sad that we had no better tools to care for our children or ourselves. We should've called the police for help, but through the years we'd seen what little help they offer in domestic disputes – incest being a dispute no one wanted to touch.

What about the church? Oh, we couldn't share the truth there. That's where my father went for help.

We believed there was nowhere else to turn. Our money spent, the only funding we had left was my brother's credit card, which was about to max out.

With the children safely away from their fathers, they started to open with stories of abuse. All we had was time in that motel room. My oldest told me of a time that she got out of the bathtub and went to lay on the couch with her father. She was naked and wrapped in a towel. She shared that he rubbed her vagina and touched her. My sister's youngest boy shared that his father tried to push his penis through his underwear when they were lying in bed together. Her oldest boy's physical signs on his body were why we were on this trip, so we knew his story held weight.

I decided to call Richard and ask for help. If he could be honest, maybe he could confirm some of the details of abuse my daughter was laying out. He confirmed the story of lying on the couch with her. He promised we would get into counseling if we came home immediately. Exhausted, out of other options and no money, all eight of us loaded into the rental car and made the long drive home to Washington.

At home, of course, Richard took his story back. But I'd come too far to let that happen without involving someone outside of the family, so I called the police. Richard was removed from the house and the kids were interviewed.

In the end, nothing came of the investigation – the girls clammed up and Richard was cleared of any charges. Richard returned home and I sank into a world of despair. He told me Brit's story on the road was because of my fucked-up past. That if I hadn't been through abuse as a child, Brit would never have heard these stories and then created her own. I did not discuss my father's sexual abuse of me with my children. Anything they heard had to be secondhand, but I succumbed to his erroneous lies. I told him at that time, if I was this messed up, he needed to take my children and get them safely away from me. He told me he'd stay and love me.

I had been taught to believe -- if there was a problem – I was the problem!

Here are the words from my oldest child, as she writes to our family about this event seventeen years later:

> If you want to blame my mom for anything blame her for doing what she did next. She stayed. She suppressed the knowledge of the[sexual] abuse because it was too painful for her to confront. Because of this, the abuse my sister and I endured continued for many years. Until I was 14 to be exact. At this point I came to my mom again and told her what my dad had been doing to me. This time she left for good.

I was bad. The words of abusive, controlling people dictated my world. Unbeknownst to me, my children continued to be sexually abused through the years, and more severely than before. This was my reward for believing in my frailty and being convinced by yet another liar that I was the one to blame. I was the crazy one. I handed more power to my ex-husband, and he used it.

Years after our divorce he told me and the girls, "I could do anything to your mother."

And he could. I should have taken more care of what I chose to believe about who I was, and what my children and me deserved.

We built a house in Oregon in 1998. By now, I was very estranged from my family of origin. I rarely saw my grandmother or Uncle Dick – who was my favorite. All my siblings had gone in different directions. No one trusted each other.

On a rare occasion, we had my mom over for Thanksgiving in our new house. Mom, my oldest sister, and her husband, Tim, joined. The turkey was great, the pies were perfect, and then I threw mom out of my house.

Longing for family connection, I reached out to them. I was excited when they accepted my invitation. We had just built a beautiful custom home and I was proud of it. After dinner, I fired up our laser disc karaoke system. I was in the middle of a song when my mother screeched like a stuck hog. I turned off the song and she was attacking Tim. Mom had launched into a saga about how she had our backs with Dad. Tim is a quiet man but couldn't keep silent listening to her bullshit. He adamantly told us how he'd heard her talks with our father, and she wasn't telling the truth. She stood squarely in front of him, her finger in his face, screaming, "You're a worthless piece of shit!" I told her she'd have to leave. I didn't want my children exposed to this shit show. We had enough crap in our lives already.

I had watched a documentary about the holocaust called *Hitler's Children*. It helped me grasp how families respond to horrendous pasts. Most couldn't stay with the truth. Rather, they moved into strict denial of the events. Others, less often, were courageous enough to stay with the true horrors and heal.

Unfortunately, my brother and oldest sister later recanted their stories and couldn't commit to the truth of the sexual abuse we received.

The book *Trauma and Recovery* by Judith Lewis Herman says it best, "The conflict between the will to deny horrible events and the will to proclaim them aloud is the central dialectic of psychological trauma."

To stand with our truth would prove to take more courage than the rest of my family could find. I would be on my own, again.

Things continued to get worse in my marriage and in our home. I began family meetings with Richard and the girls. I was going to church and staying in counseling. What I was learning, I was determined to teach my family. I read the book *Boundaries* and would give an example lesson at each meeting. Inevitably, the meetings ended with Richard getting angry and saying, "This is a bash Dad time and I'm not staying for it."

That was okay. I was trying to teach my girls that they had the right to leave the room if their father spoke abusively to them. I told them to refrain from being disrespectful and just walk away.

During this time, Richard raped my oldest daughter. That was how well these meetings and setting boundaries with evil worked. Richard, Brit, and I were all standing in the kitchen one morning. He reached out to her playfully. She shrunk away from him instantly. Her eyes flooded with hate for him. Disdain lurked behind her absent voice and then she shot out, "Don't touch me."

I knew in that moment I should not have believed him all those years ago when he had convinced me that if there was a problem, I was the problem. He was still sexually abusing my girls and I had to get out. This religious approach of kindness and setting boundaries without implementing a consequence for violating those boundaries just wasn't ever going to work.

The Spirit of Religion had fooled me again. My shame kept me hidden behind the very cloak my father hid behind.

I was thirty-five and barely functioning by this time. We had a very profitable business, a beautiful home, anything I could want – a boat, four-wheelers, clothes, jewelry, you name it, we had it. Yet, there was nothing but chaos and rotting souls within our house and I could no longer deny it. I had been in counseling for some time, read as many books on self-help as I could absorb, and looked for my escape. We needed out of this seventeen-year term in Richard's prison, and I wasn't going to stop until we were free. Even if it cost me my life.

One night, I sat on the floor of the large bathroom we had beautifully tiled. As the night hours moved past, I felt possessed with the feeling of being a small, helpless child. I picked up a pen to try to write out what I was feeling but could not. It scared me. I went to my counselor to explore these feelings with him, but he excused it as a silly, petty experience. I fired that counselor. I didn't have to have a degree to know something was stirring inside me and I needed help.

Soon, I found a new counselor. The one important thing she gave me was to tell me that if I got my children out of our house, they would have things to tell me. Then, she told me that she could no longer see me because the stories I had, and this is an actual quote, "are what happens in movies, and she didn't have the skill to help me."

I reluctantly moved on, with a depleted feeling that there was no help for me. I am thankful now that she told me to move on. She was a Catholic counselor who met with the family once. She quickly surmised after meeting Richard that I wasn't being fair with him. God help me if had listened to her and stayed in my marriage longer.

When I left him, I had almost no self-esteem. I met my second husband a few months after that.

He walked up to me, a very handsome twenty-eight-year-old man and said, "Who the hell are you?"

I looked behind me because I was certain he couldn't be talking to me.

Ten

HarmonyStar

Tears are words that need to be written."
— Paulo Coelho

My divorce was final in January 2000. I was free. Or was I? Leaving this prison, I realized I had two other POWs with me – my girls. At this point, I just wanted to be free and let us all have fun. I spent a lot of time partying. I wanted desperately to escape our reality. I was free after a seventeen-year marriage with an abusive control freak. I didn't want to explore my past or my children's pasts. But you can't outrun your past, nor can you hide from it. The anesthesia of alcohol wasn't strong enough to kill my inner drums that continued to beat with a rhythmic percussion toward the past.

It was a crazy time for all three of us. We were out from my ex's control and running without rules. I still held down a very good job. I fixed up our apartment and basked in the beauty of its feminine charms – it was mine. We had left a 3,800 square foot house and moved into an 800 square foot apartment but that didn't matter -- it felt so good to be free. Despite the happy feelings of unrestraint, I saw deep pain in my children and many mends that needed to happen for us.

The divorce decree gave us joint custody and Brooke stayed with her father. In December Brit came to me and told me she was moving in with them. On December 8, 1999, I received a call from the Clacka-mas County Sheriff's office. Richard was arrested for backhanding Brit and leaving a bruise and swelling on her face.

On January 28, 2000, I received the Clackamas County Sheriff's office report. The report indicated that after Brit was struck in the face Brooke walked downstairs to see what the commotion was and her father threw her into a wall and told her to stay out of it. It also disclosed that Brittany had told the police about the sexual abuse between her and her father.

This event opened wide the door to the hidden sexual abuse that my girls had endured with their father. I was overwhelmed, to say the least.

A temporary restraining order was placed against their father. For a short time, I had them both back with me.

As grace would have it, the Clackamas County Sheriff's office sent both girls to CARES (Child Abuse Response and Evaluation Services). They were put through a rigorous interview process, given physicals, and assigned to counseling sessions.

This began our real battle – another war against darkness.

Brooke was caught in the crossfire of her father and struggled with going between our homes. I still have the letter of June 20, 2001, where Richard's attorney writes, "Mr. White reports that your client, Ms. Jodie White, has, on more than one recent occasion, failed to allow him to have scheduled parenting time.

I never wanted to allow her to go.

My fight for both of my girls ensued.

During 2003, I opened an all-age karaoke bar, coffee shop, and restaurant at the prompting of my eldest daughter. It'd be great to open a place where my kids and other teenagers could retreat to and be safe, away from alcohol and other societal pressures. I quit drinking, cashed out my retirement, abandoned the security of my day job, and stepped full time into a new venture: restaurant by day, all-age karaoke bar by night. My oldest daughter and I had birthed this idea one day sitting in the car talking. She told me about a dream of hers to open a coffee shop geared for teenagers with loads of books everywhere. As we talked, we created a business plan and began our hunt for a location.

We found a spot (an old diner) several blocks from a local high school. It took us months to rework the inside of this old restaurant. We took the tables and created themes under a waterfall of resin that rested above the images. We painted the walls, created fun in each of the bathrooms, and designed one menu for day and a separate one for evening events. Our best-selling items were hamburgers, French fries, and an array of mocktails served in a festive glass for four!

We called it *HarmonyStar*.

Our hope was that the kid with black fingernail polish would mix n' mingle with a kid that was on the football team. The karaoke component was to give the stage to these young budding adults. A moment in the spotlight would push them into realizations that they could be somebody: seen, heard, and successful. It was successful and helped many kids.

During this time, I had both children. Brooke had a horse and spent much of her time with the 4H girls at the barn where we rented a stall. Unfortunately, by now Brit had met an older boy who would introduce her to heroin. That began another battle for her life.

I received paperwork from Richard's attorney on October 16, 2003. The paperwork is asking "to grant primary legal and physical custody of the parties' child, Brooke A. White." He also asks that his child support be suspended.

In February 2004 we closed *HarmonyStar*. I took my old job back, ended my two-month marriage to the 28-year-old, and we moved into my grandmother's attic for a short time to regroup. I was proud of my effort to give my children and the other children a place to hang but was depleted by life – struggling to be available for myself to grow and find any capacity of substance for my children.

I was happy to be at my grandmother's – the very house that had brought me comfort as a child. The years of my abusive marriage and the estrangement from my family left little time for us to be together. That changed when I left Richard. Grandma was the first person I went to. I stayed close to her until her death. Nothing was going to separate us again.

Brooke decided to live full-time with her dad because he moved to a town close to her childhood friend. I called the school district, introduced myself, and asked that I be called any time she missed school. I wanted to stay close to her as I understood the dark war. I bought her a storage box and sent cards to her weekly. I wanted her to store my love away in that box to keep the strength of love with her.

Brit turned eighteen fraught with heroin addiction, but never returned to her father. Working full-time and not knowing what drug addiction looked like, I missed the depravity of her situation.

On June 30, 2005, I filed and served Richard with custody modification papers giving me sole custody of Brooke when she was seventeen. I found out that while at her father's, he not only allowed her to use meth – he gave it to her!

He continued to harass the girls. Brooke was now eighteen. I encouraged her to seek her own restraining order against him and she did. His defense was her "bat-shit crazy mom." The judge told him he would go to jail if he continued to harass Brooke and issued a restraining order. Her dad would not be able to leave flowers on our porch anymore.

The three of us now found ourselves alone in the boxing ring of life -- battling it out together. I didn't yet have the strength to face all that would be coming in the following years, but I never got out of the ring with them.

Eleven

Finding a Guru/Finding a Murder

"Do not go gentle into that good night. Rage, rage against
the dying of the light."
– Dylan Thomas

Life has a funny way of trying to show us our past experiences. I'm sure there's someone with a fancy degree who could explain it to me, but I'm quite intrigued how my own being, and God, guided me to the real question: was I willing to put in the time and effort it would take to decipher my past? I was learning to listen to the signs and realizing the unexpected ways in which they could present themselves.

Years earlier, on a beautiful sunny Northwest day, my sister, Crissy, and I packed up our kids, loaded up an array of snacks, and headed to the river, blown-up inner tubes in tow. We picked a park on the Columbia River so we would all have an extended shoreline to enjoy. My sister and I grabbed our tubes, slathered our bodies in suntan lotion, and began our float on the tube rounds that were hot from the sun. The kids screamed and played together. It was so beautiful watching cousins enjoying each other.

Our tubs were floating and spinning as we watched the kids play. My tube spun me around and I faced away from the shoreline. My sister playfully reached her foot out to my inner tube to spring me back around and then hold me in place close with her toes.

I looked down at her feet and froze, stricken with raw panic. I kicked her away with a hard shove.

She was puzzled, to say the least. "Jodie, what's that about?"

Hell, I didn't know. All I knew was that my body went into fight or flight in that moment.

Over the years, I thought back on that day, trying to determine what had caused me to respond to her bare feet in such a primeval way. At that time, my sister and I had managed to stay close, which was a very difficult thing to do in a family like ours, but the days and hours of my life were driven by a wind to explore the past. I was not able to avoid it.

To do that, I had to be more aware of my own pain.

After some searching, I met an amazing counselor named Sara. She was the therapist who helped me initiate change and start exploring my past with tools of the trade. I had been to several counselors before her, but none like this. Sara and her cohorts believe the need to foster relationship with their clients, that the therapeutic alliance you have with your counselor can act as a model for how you may heal in other relationships as well as provide you with a safe space to explore new ways of relating. The other counselors/psychiatrists I'd seen were well-educated and book smart but helped me very little. I needed to trust someone, and Sara built that trust in me. This relationship with her began over the next many years of exploration and the courage to try.

As I said, life continues to throw curve balls at you. It isn't like, "Wow, I can tuck myself away in a room and heal." I wish it were that easy, but it isn't.

Cinnamon, an attorney I'd worked with for thirteen years, had become a close friend of mine. She was the attorney for my own divorce and a strong advocate for me through the years, as well as the first female friend I'd created. I felt privileged to have the friendship of an attorney. A woman who had been to college and now held a position of power. I wanted to model myself after women like this. She knew the story of my family and often, when I'd see them, would express how she noticed a significant and negative change in my moods afterward. She helped me in my attempt to prosecute my ex-husband when issues of abuse arose during and after my divorce. She was my advocate and it felt good.

My brother was now going through a divorce of his own and we were spending more time together. I went to meet him for karaoke one night after work and brought my good friend Cinnamon with me. They hit it off. Soon after, she told me that they were going to start dating. As you can imagine, this was a huge issue for me. The beginning of her sexual relationship with my brother began to stir in me my own sexual issues with him. I begged her to change direction, but she couldn't, and their relationship continued. This brought more of my memories to the surface and would incite a ration of shit for me to deal with. I didn't have the time, the energy, or the want to go there. Memories are stored in the brain and in the body, hidden from us, and recalled whether we ask for them or not.

As the tide shifts often, so did my attempts to regain my strength and I again tried to stop drinking at the request of my counselor and my kids. Sara told me if I wanted to heal deeper, doing so without alcohol would help and it did. One day, as I could no longer hold back the memory of my brother, I ended up at the houseboat of a friend. As the memories flooded back, I had an overwhelming feeling to vomit. I tried to suppress it, as I had done in the past, but it wasn't helping. I went to the place I knew would calm me -- a hot bath. I stepped into the water, submerged my body, and the floodgates of memory opened.

I cried and traversed the pain of yet another rape, this time at the hands of my brother. He had talked to me about these very memories in the past. I had no memory of it until that afternoon in the bath.

Both teenagers now, my brother came into my room late one night. He was trying to force his enraged penis into my mouth. This time, I just did not comply. Angry, he raped me. I minimized his abuse and hid for him constantly. I know there were many episodes with him, but I don't want to recall them with any more detail.

As God would have it, my friend Sharon came to my rescue. Coming into the bathroom, she saw my condition, hopped right in, and held me – clothes on and all. We cried some and then laughed together.

She took me out of the bath and lay with me for hours on the bed. We conversed and shared our similar experiences. She'd been sexually abused by her father, too. I'm so thankful for the people who have helped me through my life and out of those excruciating moments to a future beyond the pain. Layer upon layer the pungent odor of abuse and betrayal stung my eyes. I was on a hunt for a memory much deeper than this one, the memory with Dad and Craig in a hotel room. Unfortunately, while on the journey to that destination, I was going to have to walk, and sometimes crawl, through the fire if I wanted to find my freedom. In the end, it didn't matter how slowly I went – I just couldn't stop.

As I struggled through this time, Cinnamon and my brother were planning their wedding. Cinnamon and I met a few times to try to evaluate what this meant for our friendship going forward. We both knew it would not work. She was becoming a part of a family I was learning to stand against. It would have been sad enough just to lose her friendship, but that wasn't where it ended. I imagine she had to change the facts in her mind so she could embrace the family she was entering. In her pursuit to do this, she put on her metaphorical attorney hat and began building a case against me. She was becoming a part of my original family, and with it – as I told her would happen – she had to step into their denial.

A few weeks before the wedding, she asked to meet. Sharon accompanied me and we met Cinnamon at a local happy hour one day after work. We used to call ourselves The Three Musketeers. This day, the dynamic was different. Now, she wanted to pick me for information.

"You need to tell me everything you know about your family." Her words stung as they rolled off her tongue.

I told her I wasn't going to do that, that she needed to talk to my brother, her now finance', for that information. She pleaded. I told her if we were to meet as friends, I would open up some.

She answered, "Anything you tell me I can't say I won't use against you."

Sharon stood, crying, and said, "The only thing at this table that has changed is you, Cinnamon."

Our relationship was forever changed and so was the happy dynamic of The Three Musketeers.

Her unfounded betrayal devastated me. I had not changed in any way, but she had. My desire was ultimately that my family would speak the truth and we would heal together. Her positioning would only aid in their continued denial. As for me, it made me fight harder to stay grounded.

The issue of the motel room I remembered going to with my dad and his friend, Craig, as a child was always with me, particularly after the strange encounter I'd had twenty years earlier when my ex-husband took me to the motel on our night out, or any time I had stayed in a motel room. I'd pace the floors while my children slept, not knowing what the fuck was wrong with me. It was a strong invisible force and I needed to penetrate it to be whole.

In time, I told Sara about it. She, of course, wanted me to spend time exploring what was in that room, but I did not want to. That seems like a misstatement – I did not want to, but the truth of the matter was that I spent time staying away from it. Sara told me once that I made it harder on myself by not stopping and diving into that room. We spent many sessions trying to find a way to open the door in my mind to reveal the full detail of the motel room. I fought it. I fought this one hard. Then, one day, I felt as if I were going to lose my sanity. The harder I tried to keep the ugliness of that room hidden, the more it would mock me.

My children were home this Saturday afternoon. The sun was out and the last thing I wanted was to recall a memory. Seriously? Would you want to waste a beautiful Saturday on that? Neither did I but a strange phenomenon was happening. It felt like my mind was splitting and I couldn't hold it together. I was so frightened that I had to call Sara.

She answered and I told her that she needed to send in some men in white jackets to collect me at my house. My understanding of reality was in upheaval, and I was scared.

Sara and I continued our work over the phone. We had to if I was going to make it through that day. I can still feel the panic that I was losing my sanity.

Sara asked if there was any place I could go in the house to be alone. She assured me that I wasn't losing my mind but needed to get to a quiet place.

I went to my bedroom, closed the door, and lay down on the bed. My heart was pumping with anxiety. She told me I'd be fine and explained that my adamant denial of the memory was making the situation worse. This time I was willing to listen. Next, she asked me to walk through an exercise with her. She told me to find something in the room that I could focus on. Directly above me on the ceiling was a fan -- I would place my focus there. She told me to make no judgments about what I was seeing, but just to describe to her what it was.

I started with, "I see fan blades. It is white. There are screws."

Right beside the ceiling fan, my mind's eye saw the inside of that motel room almost instantly. There was my father, Craig, and some blonde woman. My father slit the woman's throat and ended her life. I explained this to Sara as I was seeing it. My soul began to empty some of the fear and violence I experienced that day some thirty years earlier.

I froze as the memory of witnessing that murder spewed out of me.

As daily life resumed, this discovery was almost more than I could bear, and I often wanted to escape. Normal life continued at its dulling speed, with all its demands. I had my children who needed care through their scars, too. I was not functioning at a high level but managed to keep my job.

There was still this issue with Cinnamon. We both still worked together. I would have debilitating flashbacks at night, pull myself together, and walk into work the next day -- my face not betraying the horrors that kept me from sleep. To make matters worse, gossip and rumors about my childhood had begun swirling at work. A co-worker explained how Cinnamon was telling them why I didn't accept her pending marriage to my brother. Life could not have been more complicated. I had always seen my job as a place of safety. A place of retreat to forget reality and focus on the task at hand. Now, however, my personal life and my work life had collided.

Cinnamon never quit her pursuit to discount me from every angle at work. I could take no more. Sara told me that I didn't have to go through this. What a revelation! I didn't have to endure pain and mis-treatment. She told me that I could get a doctor's release to take some time off. She wrote my doctor a detailed letter about my situation, and he gladly agreed to help. He sent the note to my employer, and I never went back. I hired an employment attorney to defend me, and we settled. I received a great settlement and Cinnamon lost her job at the law firm we worked at.

As if trying to find all the pieces of your past isn't hard enough, you always have the added burden of the circumstances. I did not begin life with a lot of belief in my intrinsic value. My father's distorted pride came through his vocal cords and bellowed, "You have no rights, only privileges." Well, this mentality led my path directly to men who dic-tated the same way. The chaos of my relationships could be helpful if I wanted to be distracted from reality for a time. It also helped enforce the overwhelming feelings I had of just that -- I was bad. Bad, bad, bad. I took a deep hit of responsibility for the damage that lay in the wastelands behind me.

One night, I drove home extremely intoxicated. Honestly, I drove drunk a lot, but this night Brooke was waiting for me to see her new dog, Molly. She was aghast at the condition in which I drove, and I wanted to deflect. Drunk and laughing, I called the dog a red-headed stepchild. My kid didn't find the humor in the comment. I walked to my bedroom with more resolve than ever that I was, indeed, bad. Strange how the more I fought to find myself, sometimes it felt like what I was finding was a belief that I was a treacherous person, hiding in fear of being exposed. It sounds strange in retrospect, but now with more recollection of who I was, life threw me into a crazed tailspin. I somehow blamed myself for much of it. And, what's more, I could prove I was bad through my self-destructive behavior.

Maybe drinking too much helped me keep people away from me. I didn't want another person to explore me, especially now. They'd think I was awful or call me a liar. Holding on to any belief in myself was a daunting, daily task. I didn't have enough strength to defend my new memories to anyone. I just wanted to hide and heal.

Men in white jackets didn't have to come collect me, rather, I collected myself. Sara and I had discussed my need to call the police. And I did that same Saturday afternoon. I had to and I felt a little insane.

I told the 911 operator "I need to report a murder that I witnessed as a child in 1968 at the Riverside Motel on Highway 14.'

Twelve

Inciting Murder

"You wanna fly, you got to give up the shit that weighs
you down."
– Toni Morrison from Song of Solomon

Several months after that initial recall, I had my first flashback.
Thinking of the flashback as a clue to the next piece of work -- no
matter how painful -- I had to try to view it as a positive indication
that I was ready now and willing to remember. These flashbacks would
happen off and on through the years, unwelcomed, unexpected, and
very unwanted. Once I opened the door, they kept returning – sometimes with a vengeance.

This evening, I had my boyfriend stay over. He got up in the middle
of the night to use the bathroom and when he opened the door to
my bedroom to come back to bed, it startled me out of sleep. When I
opened my eyes, I flew up in bed, moving against the wall, and cried
out, "Are you Dad or Craig? Are you Dad or Craig?" I tried to focus,
but all I was seeing was a man in the shadows coming toward me, a car
door was opened behind him, and the headlights were shining on the
spot they had been working.

I was transported to that Saturday night in June: Dad and Craig had
been working all day and I had fallen asleep in the back of the car. In

the latter half of the day, we were in a different car. This car was gold, had two doors, and a black interior. They opened the door, and someone was climbing in the back. It scared me. Then, I could see that it was my dad. He crawled in and collapsed in the back seat with his head landing on the top of my legs. I was so small it was suffocating.

This flashback had not only showed me that we had used two cars, but that it was very late at night by the time we arrived back home. It also confirmed that they had buried the body on my parents' property in, what would later become, the family dumpsite.

The flashback freaked my boyfriend out so bad, he got dressed and walked out of my house at 3:00 a.m., leaving me scared and alone. No man would want to love me while I explored these dark waters. Maybe my mother was right when she told me, "Good thing God made you beautiful because after all you've been through no man is going to want to love you." I was frightening for them and just too much. I did have my God and my children and that was enough.

Sometime after the flashback, I knew I had to lodge a formal complaint with law enforcement. This was in 2005. I believed in myself enough to write the following letter:

To whom it may Concern:

I am going to give you my statement about a murder that occurred in 1968. I am sure this is an unusual type of letter. I write it after much thought and heartache. I do not take these coming words lightly and understand the penalty of a false report.

I am now 41 years of age. My name is Jodie White. I state, as follows:

Remembering....The day is sunny. I am driving with my father in a light blue--silver car, it has four doors. My father, James Stanley Steele, is driving and I am sitting in the passenger's seat. We drive for a short distance and pull into a small motel. We park and my Dad puts me in a white, plastic chair on the sidewalk of the motel. He is gone for a short time. I remember looking across the road and seeing railroad tracks on a hillside. I can remember dangling my feet off the chair and then I hear a bit of a commotion and I see a lady. My Dad returns and takes me by the hand and leads me to a room. I see a woman outside and she is not happy about something, I don't know what. Dad is mad with me and spanks me. He then leaves the room and comes back in, even more mad now. He's pacing, and he is upset. Within a very short time, his friend, Craig Holbrook, comes into the room with a blonde woman. She is wearing a skirt and top and she is fighting him.

Reading this very early memory now reminds me how far I still had to go. Should I have waited the years it would take to get more recall before I sent in my statement? It was certainly a crude initial entry to this murder, but it helped me. This very first memory never changed, but much would be added it to it.

The letter continued:

She's yelling and trying to get away. Craig says nothing. He walks her in and immediately walks over in front of a small nightstand with a light on it. The bathroom door is behind them to the right. There is a window right before the bathroom door. The bed is right next to them on the left. I am sitting on the floor at the foot of the bed on the left--hand side. Dad is beside me. The door directly behind him – a little to the right. Craig turns around in front of the nightstand and holds the lady's arms down, hard. She cannot move, he's a very big man. With her arms held firmly in place by Craig, my dad walks over to her and cuts her throat, deep. She does not scream but goes limp. There is blood everywhere on her, but mostly in her long hair. Dad moves back a bit and picks her up by her ankles and they lay her down on the floor. I can see her feet coming out from the side of the bed, but that's all I can see of her. She is not moving.

Dad goes into the bathroom and washes. He walks out and they pick her up and put her on the bed. They wrap her up in the bedspread. Dad goes outside and comes back in. They carried her to the back of the car and put her in the trunk. I am in the back seat, Dad is driving and Craig is in the passenger seat and I think crying. I can remember heading down the Camas highway to our new house, but don't remember a lot until . . .

Being woke up by Craig, its nighttime and we are now in a two--door car. It's dark outside and I don't know where Dad is. The car was parked at the bottom of the hill and they were working to the right of the car doing something. We headed for home.

I knew what they were doing right down to the cars they were driving and how they hauled the body to the burial site. I couldn't say it like that then. I was leading myself – painstakingly I might add -- through this whole process to prove my memories valid.

I continued:

> That is the end of my statement. After this memory, I have since talked to my family. My father says there is no evidence. I have found out the following facts that I hope are helpful.

> FACT: My grandmother worked at Riverside Inn Motel. I was not aware of this until I spoke with my mother. She said she cleaned rooms there in 1967--68.

> FACT: My grandmother drove a blue--silver Oldsmobile in those days, four doors. Her name was Edna Steele and she was married to James Steele. Later, that car was given to my cousin, Steve Head, in the 70s. The car would have been registered. Can you still trace blood?

> FACT: If he had gramma's car, he probably had the keys to the motel.

> FACT: My parents drove a gold car, with two doors.

> My mother was amazed that I could have any idea of any of this.

> FACT: Craig Holbrook is a witness. He was there with us. His brother lives at: 26130 NE Rawson Road, and his name is Barry. Barry said that Craig recently relocated to a small town in Washington called Onalaska.

> FACT: We were building our house in 67--68, but mom told me we moved in around 11/68. I know our house was not done, because we returned to our home in Vancouver, on Delaware Lane. My parents live on 40 acres and have since 1968. I am sure Dad buried her body there.

> FACT: There is a dump site on my parents' property. Dad, for years and years, put everything in this big hole. Washers, dryers, and garbage and garbage and garbage, until the hole was filled. Property 20 years later, he

got garbage service. Mom always wondered why. I think she (the body) is under it all. It is the exact place I remember them working at that night, I remember when I awoke... by the headlights that were on in the car.

FACT: There is one missing woman on Washington Patrol's list from 1968. She was last seen 10/68, right before we moved in. Her name is Verla Winter. What happened to her?

Of course, a few years later I would get the hospital records, which would give me the exact date. With that date, I would find a seemingly real victim -- I hoped. I closed the letter with my summation of the work I had done thus far:

What I can piece together makes some sense. Dad had grandma's car, I don't know why. He probably had her keys, which had the motel keys on it. This would have given Dad and Craig time to go back and clean up, after dumping the body. Then, we probably gave grandma's car back and got ours —the two door I woke up in. I don't have memory of all this, only bits and pieces of the day after this all happened.

Mom does remember one day the three of us working very, very late at the property. He's a diabetic and she remembers that night only because he ended up in the hospital. There is probably a record of that too, which would give us a date.

I don't know if there is any we can do at this point, but I felt I needed to share this in case somebody, somewhere has a missing person and they don't know why.

I will do anything to help. This is my declaration under penalty of perjury. I understand fully the consequence of false reporting and am making my best effort to tell the truth.

My long career in a law firm directed me to add the declaration at the end of my letter. I wanted them to know, beyond a reasonable doubt, I believed my memory was accurately represented to them.

This was enough for law enforcement. They believed me enough to open a case -- Vancouver Police Department Case No. 06-17083.

Obviously, I'd welcome any opportunity to escape the existence of these memories and now having them constantly interrupting my life. One night, I was visiting with a neighbor on my back patio. She smoked a lot of pot. I didn't smoke pot, but at her insistence, I tried a puff. I got so high that I was no longer apart of the conversation but found myself floating to the top of the umbrella that graced the patio table. Up I went and then back to my seat I was plummeted. After a few minutes of this up and down journey, I had a plan -- I'd hold my ear lobes down to maintain some gravity in my chair. It worked until someone brought me back to reality by asking me why I was holding my ear lobes. Through much laughter that night ended, but the pursuit to find all I could did not.

This is my journey for the next eight years. I will try to deliver the story of how it happened for me, not leaving anything out, should someone accuse me of not telling the truth. And so, I do not hold myself in contempt. These were grueling years. One visit with Sara during this time, I asked her if she could put me in a category, a mental illness category. Asking her, "Why don't you just categorize me, give me a little pill to take for the rest of my life, and I'll walk away and live on?"

She told me she could not. She asked if I wanted to see the chart they used to diagnose mental illness. We looked at it together. The closest category my symptoms fit was OCD, but she couldn't fully diagnose me into that category. She said she could not slot me into any category other than PTSD. Being mentally ill would have been easier to deal with than these memories, the person I was because of it, fighting against my family's plea that I stop, and the agony of trying to forgive.

I had confronted my father. Now, I would confront Craig, his lifelong friend and co-conspirator. Craig most likely had Dependent Personality Disorder. Folks with this disorder often agree to things they feel are wrong or dislike to avoid being alone or losing someone's support. This was the friendship I saw between them. Maybe Craig's tears after the murder supported my theory. After all, I was their little buddy.

This letter is dated June 14, 2005, the letter Craig's nephew and his wife called me about. I wondered if he would help me.

> *Dear Craig:*
>
> *This letter may come as an unexpected voice from the past. I know you will remember me. I am Stan Steele's youngest daughter, Jodie.*
>
> *As the years have gone by, I have found this part of me that compels me to the past. I am not writing you to charge you with anything, nor am I writing to confront you with anything. A lot of things happened in my early years with my father, and I was wondering if you had any interest in helping me.*

Now, Craig was at our home when we were being molested as children and he was with us when the murder happened. I didn't write about the sexual abuse. I wanted to stay at a fair perimeter with him, testing to see if he'd answer. I continued:

> *I thought you might be interested in talking with me because you seemed to have a sense of fear towards Dad too, you weren't as cruel as he was, and he definitely was the ringleader in those days, even with you. I am just searching for some peace. I have tried to speak with him about this stuff and he just tells me it is "not good for me," etc., etc.*

I read many books trying to understand how to heal, move forward – why people did such acts. This one book I read, called *The Power of Confession,* talked about the freedom people exhibited while telling something they'd never told before. I continued my letter:

> *I wonder what you remember about the Riverside Inn Motel right off of the Camas freeway. I don't want to say any more about it in a letter but would love to discuss this with you in person or by phone. I know that soon after that time you didn't visit our new home anymore, and the last time I saw you was in front of the fridge – You leaned over and said hello......can't remember if you had Certs with you that time or not......seems like it was another treat....but, I don't remember seeing you since 1968.*

I wanted him to know that I knew. The Certs were his signature candy for us children (which years later he'd tell me he didn't remember). I remembered. I wanted him to feel the threat of what my words meant but what an outlandish idea, really. I had the brittle fear of that little girl build up in me each time I reached out to Dad and Craig to tell them I remembered. I feared that my safety could be in jeopardy. This wasn't an easy time.

> *If you would be willing to help me, and maybe help find some peace yourself, please call me. I did not tell mom or Dad that I was writing to you....I seldom speak with either of them but I know they would not agree with my decision to contact you. But, I thought maybe you would be willing to talk. If you are, please call me at (503) 422--5888. I live in Vancouver and we could meet for a drink or chat by phone.*
>
> *Thank you for at least considering my offer.*
>
> *Jodie*

Duh! What did I expect his answer to be? He never replied. However, years later, he would show that letter to the police when they came to see him about a missing-person case. He knew their visit was about me. That he kept that letter all those years was significant to me. What sane, innocent person wouldn't respond? He would. A guilty man would not.

Sara asked me to explore the memories I had by writing them down. Oh geez. I didn't want to do this exercise. I went home, opened a bottle of wine, put it beside me, and started writing. I never wanted anybody with me during these times. Exploring deep pain requires no one else. Plus, I was scared of what they'd think. What if I screamed or cried or exploded in grief? No, I would have to do this alone. That was really the only thing I knew – alone.

I still have the notes from that exercise on a yellow piece of legal pad. My journey continued as I wrote the words.

I then drew a diagram of how I remembered the setup of the scene in the parking lot. It was particularly odd that the car, as I remember it, was parked at an opposite angle. I took that diagram, put it in an envelope and mailed it to myself. I wanted it to be proof that I was right in my recollection, or I was wrong. Later, I drove to the motel to see if their parking was set up this way, because it wasn't logical. When I got there, the angled parking was still the way I saw it in my mind's eye. I still have that silly diagram – trying to convince myself I was a true witness.

Off and on during this exercise, I cried and struggled to stay with it. I just wanted to stop and go back to life before the memory. It was so painful now – on the daily – but I kept going.

Driving to the property Craig asks, why'd ya do it?

I was trying to piece together what happened that fateful day in June. As I'd remember, I would have an uncontrollable rush of emotions that followed. Ugh…ouch. Couldn't I just stop doing this? I hated it, but at the same time I wanted to know. I needed to know.

My legs were so little – so very little. I could so easily be disregarded. So little – I'm not safe. I need to get bigger. I'm so little.

Then, I write: D E A T H with a large period, underlined three times. It was the word I wrote on the wall in my adolescence. It saddened me deeply to understand my behavior back then. Why didn't someone, my parents, ask me what the hell was wrong with me? Why didn't they explore the nature of such a message? I was so angry with them for allowing my existence in this prison that only they held the keys to.

Years later my mother and I shared this email exchange about the incident:

June 21, 2005: Good day, Momma.

How is your day? Last night I was reading this book that I'm really enjoying....anyway, I remembered the time I wrote, with pencil, on the wall right above the entry way "D E A T H" and punctuated it with a knife. Do you remember? The police were called, etc. I did that. Did I ever tell you that was me? I can't remember, but all seems to make sense to me now.

June 21, 2005: Hi, Sweetheart: Yes, I do remember when you did that and also when you confessed to it years later. I have to confess too, that I had sensed at the time that you had done it but it was easier for me to not face any of the traumas you were going through. It's called selfishness and cowardice.

I am sure there is still a great deal of both in my life but this I know – I am here for you. You may not be able to receive that yet, which I under-stand. My motive is sincere when I tell you I will help in any way I can. You should not bear this alone. It's so very wrong for it to have ever been your burden. Please let others help.

I loved her for forced posturing here. I realized her words were for her safety not mine. She never ceased to amaze me with her ability to lie and prevaricate.

It took me a great deal of time to explore the things that were returning.

Now my notes showed a game I used to play with my father. I loved that game. He'd take a piece of paper and make a few lines or some squiggly marks and then hand it to me. I had to complete the drawing by making something out of nothing. I did have a relationship with my father that was outside of all the abuse. It was the hardest part of this emotional riddle. I loved him. He loved me, or so I tried to hold on to. It was his love serum that kept me enslaved to his secrecy.

Surrounding the game in my notes, I had written: "RAPED, DEATH, DESCARDED, MASSACRED." And then, in a bubble I wrote "Daddy's little girl." Which, I was.

During this year, I also reached out to my father. I have always tried to be fair and give him and Craig a chance to help. Probably not the brightest idea, but I just had to try.

> *Monday, June 27, 2005:*
>
> *Me: Does mercy exist. . . Help me, please, help me.*
>
> *Dad: Hi baby (and it is written just this way) i HAVE NOT BEEN ON THE PC FOR A CUPLE OF DAYS. JUST READ YOUR EMAIL I DON'T KNOW IF IT IS FOR ME OR YOUR MOM. HOW CAN I HELP?*
>
> *Me: With the truth, Dad.....that's all, the truth.*

I didn't receive a response, so I sent another email two days later, baiting him with his own code of love, and my true heart too:

> *Me: And, I do love you...... If it were not for my great fear of you, I would have seen you more often in life. I have had to self-protect – it's all I know. I do want you to know that I love you for exactly WHO you are .....there is nothing hidden about you to me –and, I still love you. I always have, and I always will . . . you are my father ..... we had some good times together I will never forget. Like you teaching me to drive a clutch. ...making popcorn and watching movies .. your sense of humor...going to Multnomah School of the Bible together.....visiting old people....etc.*
>
> *You will probably die soon....I sometimes envy that position in life...it's almost over now. What will you think of for eternity, Dad? Love or hate?*
>
> *I love you ~ Jodie*

Dad responded later that night, in a perfectly typed email:

My darling baby girl

I also remember things we did when you were a little girl. When we went to the old folk's home in Camas and what pleasure the old people got when they saw you and your big smile. I remember the old gold miner that you and me led to the Lord Jesus and how excited he got. Then Sherm came in and baptized him and we never saw him again because he quit being a recluse and joined the rest of the old people at their gatherings.

My little girl you have been away from our Lord Jesus for so long, it is no wonder that you are so miserable. Find a church and start going to it. There is a Baptist church on 78th street that would be a good one to go to. I was their one time to go to an AA meeting and all the people that went in or came out were holding hands. I had never seen this at any other church before.

If you are interested then go out St. James to 78th and take a left turn and go about ½ mile and watch for a church sign on the left. The church is off the road about ½ block. I can't remember the name; it may be Glad Tidings. Anyway, please start going to an old-line church and keep away from these new so called churches.

I also remember when you got into trouble at school because you would not let some kids get off the monkey bars until you gave them the gospel. Become a Christian like that again my baby girl and your life will change. You will have a lot of Christian friends and Brittany and Brooke will meet some young Christian men. I have never stopped loving you and will until I die. You are welcome here anytime you wish to come, after all it is still your home. Again, I love you with all my heart.

Love Dad

My father wanted me to come back to his religion. The kind of religion that didn't allow you to speak anything of abuse. The kind of religion that keeps you muzzled in a jail. The Spirit of Religion your jailer.

About two weeks before I received this email from my father, I received another email from my mom. She said:

Sunday everything kept escalating in the morning after Barbi's call until Stan said something extremely cruel to me regarding my mother. Hurt deeply I stayed upstairs to be out of his way. Mike (my Dad's brother) came to the house about then and the two of them stayed downstairs. (That's why I thought about coming over.)

Monday morning, Stan grabbed me by the door insisting I kiss him goodbye. We had another heated discussion, I told him I'd had the last of his abuse and left the house. According to Mike, Stan went on "behaving like a real asshole" until Mike left the room. Stan was convinced I wasn't coming back – Mike said he thought so, too. When he returned to the family room, hoping to address some issues, Stan said to him, "I just took a lethal dose of insulin. I took 50 units of fast acting insulin."

Mike called 911 and they transported him to the hospital. Doctor was going to keep him on an involuntary commitment for three days. Stan that afternoon managed to convince the mental health people that it was all a mistake and Mike had mistaken what he said. When I got to the hospital, Stan said, "All this trouble about me taking five extra units of insulin." Mike was so angry with him that he wouldn't ride in the ambulance and wouldn't see him until late afternoon.

A little manipulation, do you suppose? I find it impossible to believe that Mike would be wrong about what was said.

My father was still the same man he'd always been. His religion did nothing to change him, it just helped him hide. I wrote him a few more emails, with no response. This avenue was dead just like the man I attempted to cajole mercy from.

Either by fate or stupidity, I continued my fight to find the truth of my past. I just had to, for me. This was not to see Dad or Craig go to prison. There wasn't a lot of retribution in my steps toward justice. I just wanted it made right -- for the woman in the ground buried and her family, for me, and my family. So, nothing stopped me from looking, and look I did.

My first attempt at finding this missing woman was to write to the Washington State Patrol. On May 16, 2005, I sent in this:

> *Is there any record of a crime being reported, or a possible crime, at*
> *The Riverside Motel, 4400 Columbia House Blvd., Vancouver WA, in 1967*
> *or 1968 – I'm thinking Spring/Summer. Or, is there a report of a missing*
> *woman in her 20s – blonde, missing around that time.*

The information in this request came only from my memory. I knew the day was warm and sunny. Where I come from, this had to be spring or summer. I knew the lady who had been with us was blonde. The only information the State of Washington had was for a woman who went missing in October 1967. Her hair was dark. This was not the victim, but it was all I had to go on at this time.

In April of 2006, I contacted Southwest Washington Medical Center to ask for the release of Dad's hospital records. Five months later, I received a faxed release form that my father had to sign. Mom had pursued Dad to finally sign the release for the medical records. She said she had to tell him she was going to leave him if he didn't sign it. I brought the release (which took me a year to get) to the hospital to obtain the records. The lady took the release and disappeared. She came back and, offering me the envelope, held it but did not release it to me until she looked in my eyes and said, "You're not going to believe this, but these were in a box marked to be destroyed next week. I hope you find what you're looking for."

Those records gave me the date I needed – the date of the murder would have been June 8, 1968.

I scoured Dad's hospital records for anything I could find. The first thing I looked at was his time of admittance. After the flashback of the gold car, I knew it was nighttime. Right there, on the admittance sheet, was the time, "12:55 am." Diagnosis: insulin reaction. It took the hospital seven days to stabilize his condition. Never before this time, nor after, did my father require this kind of medical attention. He almost lost his life trying to cover up the life he'd just taken.

I entered that date into the local missing-person database and searched in Washington and Oregon. No match. Sometime later, I wrote to the *Cold Case Cowboys*. Their tips held that often dates and missing persons are not matched because people often need to look outside of their area. Bingo! I searched the entire US, and there it was – a woman who went missing from Venice, Los Angeles County, California in June 1968. Madeline Anna Babcock. She had dainty features (as I remembered) and her hair was blonde. My facts had found her.

I had to put her in the state of Washington (her location at the time of the murder) to prove my theory and demonstrate the accuracy of my memory. I located and then scoured the website that her sister had put up in dedication to her. One of the sites was simply titled: *Where is Madeline?* Her sister wrote:

> *As best that I can recall I do believe it was in June 1968 that Madeline (Lynn) called my mother. We had a small disagreement. I just happen to be at my mom's home when she did call. It was a really sunny day and it was I think either a Friday in late June or a Saturday?*

The day the murder happened was a Saturday, June 8, 1968. That was a match. I kept reading:

> *Mom told Lynn I was there she asked if she wanted to talk*
> *to me she said no she was at a phone booth and would see*
> *us the next day. The next day and went we called her home*
> *number later that day no answer. Mom called the following*
> *day and still no answer. Mom was very upset it was not like*
> *Lynn to call and then not show up.*
>
> *My sister had a problem drinking at the time, and could*
> *pull something like this once in a while but she was usually*
> *always prompt! Or would call and say she was delayed.*

I stopped reading. This description seemed to fit what I remember of her. Of course, they didn't hear from her because she had been buried on my parents' property. So, I had the fact that she was blonde, that she was indeed a drinker -- what else could I find?

Amid my dig for the truth, my mother stopped by my house to see how I was doing. I explained that I thought I found the woman. She asked me to show her the memorial website. As we explored it, we came across some letters her sister had attached to the website that were penned by Madeline herself. One of the letters was dated February 14, 1965. In part, she explained:

> *I wrote to Judge Rakow and explained to him why I left,*
> *and told him that I would get the allotment check cashed and*
> *send him the money for Kathy and Butch.*

My mother was a court reporter and had been in the Washington court system for years. She exclaimed, "Jodie, Judge Rakow is a judge in Goldendale, Washington." That easily gave Madeline ties to Washington state. The highway that leads her from California to her children and her old life was – you guessed it -- Highway 14. Riverside Inn Motel, the site of the murder, was located right off that highway.

I told her that I remembered her not having a car. If she had a car, we would have needed to dispose of it. This was a logical deduction as an adult. And believe it or not, in another attached document to her website, was a Missing Persons Inquiry Form from The Salvation Army. At the very bottom of the form was another piece to my puzzle. They asked for her driver's license number. In the blank her sister had written "NEVER." Another staggering piece that helped me believe I wasn't just a liar. I hadn't created any wild imagination for attention, as my family tried to convey.

My mother feigned loyalty to me, but she never held up to it. When the investigating officer met with her and my oldest sister, Karen, they produced a file for him that they and Cinnamon had created. The file was a compilation of accusations against my sanity and credibility. Never seeing the file, I cannot know what it contained. He met with them longer than he met with me.

The images that were returning to me were, in fact, the story I had lived, but buried to survive.

With all these recalls returning, I couldn't predict where or when I'd find one next. I'd try to continue living like the guy next to me -- making dinners, watching movies -- but my life had now been forever altered.

This night Brittany and I were watching a great flick and enjoying our evening. A car chase through the woods kept us on the edge of our seats, anticipating the next move. Next, the top of the car was ripped off and the pursuit continued. An unseen wire was stretching across their path, and it sliced the throat of the female.

I froze. I absolutely stiffened to being immobile. The longer I tried to block it and move on, the stronger the image perused me. My breathing became difficult. I was having a hard time even moving. After a minute or so, I told my daughter I needed help. I told her to call my counselor post haste. All the strength I could muster was not moving me past this terrifying place.

My daughter got Sara on the phone. A good counselor can save your life, let me tell you.

She said, "Jodie, what's going on?"

I replied, "We were watching this movie and the woman's throat was slit and now I can't breathe or physically move."

She asked me what image was stuck in my head.

"My Dad cutting the throat of the woman."

She proceeded to skillfully talk me off the ledge of fright, explaining what was happening to my mind and body. She said, "You're seeing a snapshot of the room you were in. That snapshot holds with it all the emotions, too. You feel stuck because you're stuck in the snapshot and the feelings surrounding it."

Once it was explained -- what my body was doing in response to the memory -- my breathing started to return to normal and the fear began to subside. I hung up but was gripped by this experience for the rest of the night.

Despite the challenges of waking up each day with a new section of my mind open, I chose to continue my efforts and kept exploring this missing person's website. Her sister gave a wealth of information that helped my pursuit. She mentioned Goldendale and White Salmon, Washington. I drove to Goldendale, which is about a three-hour drive from where I live. My purpose was to obtain her divorce records because they would be public record. I got a copy of her entire divorce file. The papers painted the picture of a woman who very likely could have been drinking in a motel room with two strange men. In the Findings of Fact and Conclusions of Law dated June 23, 1965, signed by Judge Rakow, were these words:

> That the defendant [Lynn] has been guilty of cruel and inhumane treat-
> ment rendering plaintiff's life burdensome in the following extremes, to wit:
> That the said defendant, without provocation, willfully and intentionally
> deserted and abandoned the plaintiff and the minor children aforemen-
> tioned and has in effect absconded into the state of California for the purpose
> of association with another man on an improper basis and for improper
> purposes; further, that t he said defendant during the parties' married life

has been addicted to a violent temper and as a result thereof has flown into
frequent rages and chased the plaintiff around the house with a butcher
knife, all of which has made it impossible for the plaintiff to any longer live
with the defendant as her husband.

I worked in family law for thirteen years and understood that with Lynn's absence, her ex-husband could represent to the court whatever he wanted. Although, I also knew if she left her family and children behind there was probably some truth here. I don't write those words to condemn any of her actions, simple to show how it led me to believe this description bore a strong resemblance to the woman I met. I remembered her to be a yeller, screaming her right to be heard. Her divorce records show her strong ties to her children just hours up the freeway from the motel.

The woman who was in the room with us that ill-fated morning was not timid or mild-mannered. She had been waiting for my father because she had anticipated his arrival when we pulled up to the hotel that morning. She walked up to me with a smile. She felt welcomed to be with them and seemed happy to be meeting me. She didn't show any shame and displayed no reason to shy away from me. When my father began to attack her, she didn't stop fighting until her death.

I continued to unearth valuable information to help the case. I researched weather reports from June 8, 1968. The day was sunny with a light breeze. I went to the local library and found a copy of *The Columbian*, a local newspaper. Friday, June 7, 1968: Vancouver area: cloudy Saturday morning brief sunny periods afternoon; highs in seventies; lows in fifties.

Then, from another online resource, the Weather Source had recorded precipitation for that day as 0.00. The day was sunny and dry. Okay, now I can trust that piece of my memory from the day of the murder. I called a real estate company and requested the deed on the motel property for 1968. I received a copy of the Assignment of Contract signed July 10, 1967. The property had been deeded to the Counts

-- another piece of information that I may be able to use. I then pulled up the business name to research the properties' history of owners. The name from '67 still appeared. Could we find this family and ask who ran the place in '68? This was a grasp for, ultimately, nothing that helped, but, at that time, it helped me – just to continue the search.

Next, I ordered a copy of the contract on my parents' land. If it was as Mom said, they purchased the property in 1967. A copy of that warranty deed states that my parents took possession of the land July 17, 1967. The Clark County property information showed the year that the house was built as 1968. All those dates were consistent. Dad did own the property during 1968.

I had gathered a lot of information but felt like I needed help beyond my capabilities. I also continued my full-time job in a new law firm, was trying to raise my kids, and simply didn't have full time to invest in this search. So, I hit the internet in search of a good private investigator. One site offered services for missing persons and death investigations. His name was Chris Peterson.

Chris told me he had thirty years as a homicide cop. That was enough of a reason for me to agree to meet in person.

He told me when I first called him, he thought I was a nut job, a bored housewife, but was intrigued enough to hear me out. I had a compilation of material facts that I had organized thoroughly and placed in a binder. After hearing my story and walking through all that I'd found, he heard a sincerity and credibility in it all and decided to take the case.

He half-heartedly laughed and said, "Jodie, I think you went into the wrong profession. Your facts seem to have found the missing person."

Chris told me and my mother at an initial meeting that it was one of the worst stories he'd heard a child living through. I so appreciated his sentiment. I hadn't received much acknowledgment in the past. When a survivor of any childhood trauma comes out and speaks, the horror of what you're met with is almost unbearable. I wasn't offered a hug, a kind word or understanding. Rather, I was given judgment and denunciation.

The folks who want to live in denial of their own truths, want to silence you. Your testimony makes the most righteous want to hide and the betrayal of a society that actively looks the other way is excruciatingly painful. My own family put together a file to shut me up.

The PI told me a story about a murder investigation he had worked on. They discovered, through deductive analysis, that the murder weapon was a cue ball in a sock. They suspected the sock had been thrown into a local river. Without it, they didn't have a case.

He said, "We found that sock with the cue ball," making the point that even the most unlikely cases could be solved no matter how impossible it seemed. He was clearly telling me: do not give up.

One of the first things he suggested was that we run an ad in the local newspaper. Maybe somebody remembered something from that time, but more importantly, he hoped it would put pressure on my father and Craig.

On Tuesday, May 1, 2007, the newspaper ad was published:

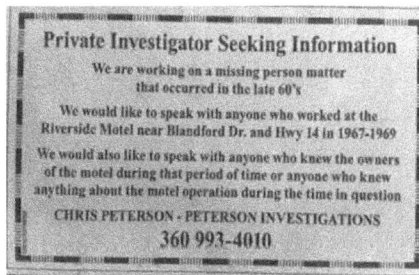

Private Investigator Seeking Information

We are working on a missing person matter that occurred in the late 60's

We would like to speak with anyone who worked at the Riverside Motel near Blandford Dr. and Hwy 14 in 1967-1969

We would also like to speak with anyone who knew the owners of the motel during that period of time or anyone who knew anything about the motel operation during the time in question

CHRIS PETERSON - PETERSON INVESTIGATIONS
360 993-4010

We received no response, but it felt good. I hoped, as the PI said, that Dad or Craig saw the damn thing.

I was a force to be reckoned with – I hoped.

Thirteen

An Olympic Race

"People often claim to hunger for truth, but seldom like the taste when it's served up."
A Clash of Kings by George R. R. Martin

During these years, a dream stuck with me. Through a colorless haze, I was a spectator at an ancient arena, somewhat like the Roman coliseum. I was sitting on the sidelines watching this epic race. For some unknown reason, the race had been going on for years. In fact, the people had been running this race for so long that all their hair was long and gray. They were dressed like Romans in white robes, tied at the waist with leather sandals elaborately strapped to their feet. Hundreds were on the track.

As I continued to watch them go 'round and 'round and 'round, a man walked up to me. He had been in this race longer than anyone. His hair was gray in color, his eyes were soft blue, and he had a beard that was unkept and very long. He'd been in the race so long that his beard was glistening with ice. It seemed this detail wasn't an indication of coldness but more that he was deeply weathered.

He walked up to me and stood still for a minute or two. Then he looked right at me and said, "Get back in the race."

I woke up and immediately knew what the message of the dream was. I had to carry on no matter what the cost. Absolutely exhausted, I had just come out of a very abusive seventeen-year marriage, broken, I believed, beyond repair. I had no idea what lay ahead of me but the battle to get out of that violent marriage had drained me. The prison of my childhood and then the confinement of my marriage had taken my self-worth, courage, and my will to go on living at times.

If I had known then what I know now, I would have looked at that man in my dream and told him I can't. I just can't. I would have pleaded with him that I didn't have the will or desire to continue. I had no idea what was next but got the message deep in my soul that I had to stay in the race and keep trying. God was with that man in my dream, and He was with me.

A hard part of the race has been to believe that I have the right to be away from evil. Far away. That I could remove myself and my children and not have guilt around that. Most god-fearing folks always put this horrific spin around forgiveness. They believe, and did not hesitate to tell me, that to be in God's will I must forgive. I believe wholeheartedly in forgiveness. What I do not believe in is the way that advice would have kept me and my children forever bound to our abusers through shame and guilt. I do not believe that God intends forgiveness to look this way.

God would never tell a human being to placate evil, entertain it, and try to make it happy. Through forgiveness, the Spirit of Religion would say, you should at least see your parents, try to understand them, be kind, compassionate, and forgive. Importantly to remember -- my parents did not ask for forgiveness. Instead, their denial flared with injustice at my accusations.

Isn't forgiveness letting go of revenge? Letting go of what you want to do to them for some semblance of justice for the pain and relentless agony they put into your life with their own hands and evil devices? I believe in this kind of forgiveness. I honor my parents by moving on and not seeking revenge. I honor them for giving me life so that I too can give life to my children. I honor that.

What I do not and will not ever honor is the evil that lurks within them. To go back to their dinner table, to meet with them at the holidays, is denying everything I believe. The truth would have to stay in my backpack, hidden away, any time I visited. When I tell the truth, I am not telling my truth. I am stating the facts. To keep them hidden would have destroyed any integrity I was building for my future. I did not need another religious façade by which to go forward. I was leaving all that behind. This religiosity teaching of forgiveness had intertwined in it this evil notion that now, when I was trying to gain my freedom, I had to give the keys back to my abusers if I was going to be Godly or good. I don't believe I have to be good. God is good. I just need to stay close to Him and He'll be my good for me. That's in the bible and I'm sticking to it. I've sometimes questioned if evil starts with, "I'm not that bad. In fact, I'm a nice person. I really am good."

Placate means to calm; to bring peace to; to influence someone who was furious to the point that he or she becomes content or at least no longer irate. This was not my job any longer. I had done that my entire childhood. I do not believe the God who sits on the eternal throne asks that of me. And I know why. You cannot silence or bring comfort to evil spirits. It is impossible. They will never have peace. Both of my parents had the presence of evil spirits. Of this, I am certain. I was also not the only one who could see this.

My oldest daughter, Brit, describes her grandparents here:

"The Devil with a baby face. As he grew older and darker, his skin seemed to drape over bone, a white-skulls face. Eyes so dark they seemed a cavern through which the night was pouring; a pinprick of red in the center, perceptible to even the smallest in the family. A physical embodiment of eternal war. He's always watching, always listening; his cold, totalitarian breath forever on your neck.

Grandma had a face filled with a desperate, yearning malevolence and had made a home where harm was the norm, where evil settled in the corners like dust. In her there was a blankness that held unspeakable darkness if one were to scratch at the surface. She was a bloodthirsty follower with remorseless manipulation honed under years of supervision from the Devil himself.

They hurled themselves upon weaker, more innocent people. A will and lust for power, for lust itself.

An Evil that would rather kill the person doing the questioning than take a realistic look at itself.

Evil colonized them."

Most could see the evil lurking in their souls – right behind their corneas was a presence that was not their own. I did not then and will not now enter a pissing match with evil. You are supposed to by biblical standards depart from evil. And that's just what I did. I also taught my children to do the same thing.

To keep people together through the guise of forgiveness with those who have miserably abused us was and is just wrong. I had every right to walk away to safety. To find peace away from them. I do not have to feel guilt or shame for not being there with them, to support them, to listen to their bullshit. I simply do not have to do that. Religious ways would tell me that I should feel the urge to care for my parents as they grow old. Help them find redemption. Okay. That's fine – fine for them.

Sure -- I had and have a lot of love for my parents, sometimes. What good is my love going to do now? It becomes a dance with the wicked.

> *Take your partner -- do--see--do, swing that bullshit 'round the floor.*
> *Don't look close or you will see, the manipulation 'round the tree.*

It just isn't possible to have an engaging, real relationship when my abusers' agenda was only to silence me. Better still, their goal was to regain their control over my mind and help me see the denial I was supposed to stay in. Reminiscent human love just isn't worth a lot to me and in truth, isn't worth a lot to them either. It's like an addiction. Your substance of choice feels great at the time, but after the initial climax, you're left with an empty feeling -- wondering why you went back.

I wasn't going to let this type of love keep me bound. I had to fight it.

Fourteen

Purgatory

"Pain Demands to be Felt."
-John Green, The Fault in Our Stars

Life around me did, indeed, go on. Wouldn't it be nice if I could have tucked myself away in a small cabin, surrounded by trees, a great lake in the distance? That's the stuff dreams are made of, but not reality.

I found myself gasping for air as work demands pressed in on me and my children needed more at times than I could give. I was drowning and just wanted to sink into an abyss. I'd fantasize about contracting some serious disease. If I were sick, I'd have to stop trying. If I had an illness that people could see, they'd understand why I was too exhausted to carry on. Someone might see why I couldn't find the strength to continue, and it wouldn't be my fault that my strength had failed me. As I sank beneath the waves, I could blame it on my health.

I wasn't the best at picking men, but men were certainly good at picking me. I'd currently found myself struggling to leave a relationship I'd been in for some time. This man cheated, used drugs, and consistently tore me down – all of which I was used to. I still hadn't found the worth to say no to this kind of treatment. In fact, during this time, I found it almost impossible to be around healthy people. I couldn't afford any more judgment of who I was or was not. So, hanging out with a cheating drug addict was somewhat easy. To be fair, he had some good things wrapped up in his package, too.

During an off time in my relationship, I began seeing someone else. My ex didn't like this and decided he'd kick open my door and take what he wanted. The man in my house was married. Separated, but still married. He wanted no part in protecting me in any way. I was on my own to fight off my intruder. Eventually, he left, and I had to phone the police for some feeling of protection. The county prosecutor's office took the case and charged him with a felony. I had just initiated an ongoing battle for the next many months.

At the same time, I was engaged in pre-trial negotiations with the firm I had worked at during Cinnamon's misconduct. While I had an employment attorney handling the case, she asked me to file a state bar complaint about Cinnamon, as this would help our case. Now, when you stand against attorneys and try to plead misconduct, it's not an easy task. But you bet I took it head-on and resolutely. I built my facts brick by brick.

During this time, Brit came to me one morning and lifted the sleeve of her shirt. She said, "Mom, look." Aghast, I looked at my precious firstborn's forearm. It was again wrought with the confusion of a heroin addiction. My precious little girl was still in a battle for her life. I could not lose her. Everything else had to stop until I could find her help. I had no time to grieve, I simply had to spring into action, though I wasn't sure what.

I started calling rehab centers, one after another. Finally, I found one in California. The research I had done told me to get her out of her current environment, so I did. I cashed out my retirement to pay for most of the cost of the facility and bought a plane ticket for her that day. The rehab center gave me a list of items that we'd need: two weeks' worth of clothes, toiletries, a toothbrush, paste, shampoo, lotions, etc., a razor (that they'd hold for her use), and heroin.

"Wait! What did you just say?"

"Heroin," came her reply. "If you don't keep her high, she won't get on the plane."

Where the hell was I going to find a bag of heroin? Alas, we found some. I gave her boyfriend money, and he secured enough for her to get well and on that plane. It was one of the hardest things I've ever had to do.

We woke up the next morning and prepared to leave for the airport. She could use one last time before we left the house. The rehab center assured me this was the only way we would get her to go. I waited downstairs while she and her friend finished the dirty deed. We got in the car, and she showed me her distorted arm. They'd missed the mark and now she had outward signs of her struggle. God, was this real!

We managed to make it to the airport and got to the gates. I could go no farther with her. She took about ten steps forward, turned around, and said, "Mom, please, I don't want to go."

Her face swollen with the years of betrayal she had lived through, it was clear her body had no strength left.

There stood my baby girl -- all the dreams and hopes I'd had for her when she was born -- now tattered by life's abuse. She barely stood. Fear gripped us both as our bitter parting could not be stopped. It took all the courage and strength she had left to turn around, face the destination before her, and leave that day. She and I both knew this wasn't an ending but another beginning. The battle was far from over.

She made it to Los Angeles and a member of the rehab center met her at the airport and drove her to her first destination, the detox center. The next day I received a call from her. She was terrified, disoriented, and feeling that I'd betrayed her. I couldn't be there to hold her, and I had never met the people caring for her. So, as Blanche expressed in the classic movie *A Streetcar Named Desire*, my daughter and I also had to learn to rely on the kindness of strangers – albeit strangers we'd paid to offer professional support.

Meanwhile, my youngest daughter, Brooke, was spending a lot of time around her father, although she stayed mostly with her best friend's family. He was a talking billboard for illicit drugs, like Ecstasy and meth, and had no problem sharing those with our daughter. At the time, my mother worked for the presiding judge of our county and always had a professional persona. She took great time and focus building her career. It empowered her personal life in many ways and helped her conceal the truest of her identities. Upon my mother's nudging, the judge she worked for agreed to meet with Brooke. I had custody of her, but she wouldn't obey the order and her dad kindly complied with her wishes. I took her to the old stone county courthouse, walked up the great staircase and into the judge's chambers, where he took her in the courtroom and sat her down at the counsel table. He took his perch on the bench. I crossed my fingers that the process of this intimidating meeting would help guide her back into safety.

Later, when she spoke about the episode as an adult, she told me she remembered feeling angry and protective of her father and the relationship that she had sought for so long with him but never got. She saw this court hearing as another impediment to achieving a relationship with him. It angered her to be there. She also wanted to disappear into that deep pool of denial with him and nourish the fantasy that he put her first. I tried forcing her to see the reality of a father giving drugs to a teenager. He was also a dangerous pedophile.

To top it off, I had a growing back issue that was becoming increasingly impossible to ignore. There were days when I couldn't stand up straight. I'd get out of the car, only to have a back spasm that would drop me to my knees. Great! Now, my body was physically betraying me. I ended up being diagnosed with a ruptured vertebra and needed back surgery. To this day, two toes are still numb, but, thankfully, I was back to my position in life and ready to carry on. I only missed about four days from work. I am a badass when I must be.

Just as an aside, during my visits to the hospital for this pending back issue, I didn't receive so much as a muscle relaxer. How the hell did the people around me have anxiety and pain drugs, a drug for this, a drug for that? I couldn't get anything. When my disc ruptured and I went back to my doctor, he deeply apologized, saying, "Jodie, I'm so sorry, I didn't know you were in this kind of pain." What do mainstream people do? Simply communicate about their pain? It didn't even occur to me to do that. If I was in his office, didn't that mean the same thing?

During this period, my grandmother died. She had been my angel, sent to save me from a life of complete despair. As I shared, her special lunches had been etched into the valves of my heart. The card games, smoking a cigarette with one in her hand and another one lit in the ashtray, playing Boggle, the vinyl spinning 'round and 'round on her old cabinet record player echoed in my soul. She was gone. Yet, another loss. I needed her. She had a way of simply being there for me – the uncomplicated and unconditional love I never received from my parents.

When I was leaving my first marriage after seventeen years, I could go to her house at 3 in the morning, open her screen door, and knock quietly on her front door. I'd wait the several minutes it would take for her to open her eyes in her back bedroom, grab her robe, and make her shaky walk to the door. I knew she would answer. There was never a time she did not. That was gone now, forever.

Obviously, life carried on -- personally, professionally, and emotionally. Every battle I had before, I still had but without my grandmother. The dark cloud that had moved upon me most of my life felt more oppressive than ever. I was desperate to find a supplement for her --maybe a good man to stand beside me as a helpmate? Not in the money sense, but someone who could aide in this heavy burden I supported daily.

I had dated a man who seemed to be from good stock, had a fantastic job, and showed interest in me and my girls. During the two years I had known him, I'd seen some bouts of anger that scared me, but all in all, I liked who he was and how he gave. After my grandmother's death, we got engaged. My mother told me if I trusted him, I should follow through with the marriage (always giving her shitty advice).

I packed my belongings (well, he packed my belongings), quit my job, and off we went to his home, now a few states away from my native territory. The relationship ended after seven weeks when he dragged me, naked, from his bed through his house one night on a rampage. It left a strawberry on the entire length of my thigh. Almost as soon as I arrived, I made the move back home where the murder investigation, the family mayhem, and the brutal course of it all awaited me. The great thing was, on the drive home, I called the firm I had been working for up until I left, and they happily brought me back. I was promoted to a new position soon after my return.

I wrote Detective Zapata to see how the case was progressing. I reminded him of the case, my father's name, and this poor missing woman who needed to be excavated and returned to her family.

You can bet I drank during this time. I consumed so much tequila, in fact, that one night, I couldn't lift my head off the floor. I had built a fire, closed the glass doors, and lay down, unable to get back up because I was too drunk. I cried out to God from the floor. The glass doors on the fireplace continued to heat up, until the right side blew out, spewing glass around me in a fiery roar. I didn't move, I just kept praying. No matter how much I drank, the pain was insatiable.

Genesis 9 holds a story about Noah. He had just come through the flooding of the earth, bringing with him his family, and leaving the rest of all that he knew behind. The bible tells us that God had to close the door on the ark because Noah would have let more in. I don't believe we can begin to know the pain and isolation of what he felt. When the ark landed and God gave His covenant through the sight of the rainbow, Noah "...proceeded to plant a vineyard. When he drank some of its wine, he became drunk and lay uncovered inside his tent." The story tells us that his youngest son found Noah naked and told his brothers. The oldest brothers covered their father up, without looking. When Noah woke up and found out what his youngest son had done to him, he cursed him. Scholars have their opinion of why Noah did this. I have mine, too. Could Noah have been so upset at his son's betrayal because of the experience he had just come through? Instead of offering to cover his father's exposed nakedness, fully vulnerable, his son brought it to his brothers' attention. I wonder if Noah felt broken hearted that his son had no compassion for this leader who listened to God when everyone mocked him for his faith. The isolation and pain that Noah had to feel as a man was relieved in those moments that he consumed the wine he had made. I get it. Too bad his son did not.

My counselor, Sara, suggested that I call the YWCA and get into a group. She felt it would help *normalize* some of my experiences. So, I did. After six weeks of baring our souls to each other in those rooms (oh, of course, I couldn't share the murder, only my sexual abuse because Sara said I needed to be careful not to vicariously traumatize others), they sent us on our way. I didn't feel like it was right to open wounds, and without any sutures, send us all away. So, I proposed that we continue to meet at a restaurant once a week. There were women who had never had sex because of the molestation, women who couldn't get enough sex, and women who just simply destroy themselves through a variety of odd addictions. After some time, we quit meeting. We were all too wounded to keep it together. I still have a cross-stitch that reads, "Full of Hope, Jodie," from one of the ladies.

Now, if I were to just leave these stories as written above, you might call me a victim. Instead, each of these victories gave me hope that I could continue no matter how small the win. I took it to heart and knew God was with me.

After months of the prosecutor's office going back and forth with my ex's attorney, here is the final verdict, taken from an email written by the Chief Criminal Deputy:

> In evaluating the overall situation, I cannot help but conclude that the conduct of Mr. Smith [name changed], considered in light of all the relevant information, is felony level conduct. Further, in considering all the circumstances, I would have no objection to a class C felony disposition that the parties might agree to, as well as an Assault 4 DV charge. Our goal here is to ensure that Mr. Smith, a first-time offender, receives some form of punishment for what he has done to insure he understands the seriousness of his conduct as well as insured that the victim is protected as allowed by law.

We all have a right to feel secure in our homes. What this defendant did here is the stuff of which justifiable homicides are made of.

. . .

This defendant by his own admissions forcibly entered a private home, this defendant clearly without provocation physically assaulted the female victim and made very derogatory statements to her during the course of the assault.

The only reason I share this email is that it was the first time I had found some justice. I was with a married man that morning, which was shameful, and would have made me do nothing against our intruder. But, because the police were called, the case was made for me by the state. How wonderful was that. I haven't seen a lot of justice from the police, so it's a great ending to a difficult story.

My daughters' various battles were the deepest battles of all. Most mothers (not mine) have a built-in mechanism to protect and save their children. Their battles were ones I truly had little control over. It was beyond devastating and the terror of not knowing if they would successfully make it out was at times almost more than I could bear. Today they are both healthy, strong, and have amazing families of their own. They are both mothers that many envy to be.

And, I still had not returned the murdered woman to her family.

Fifteen

The Woman in the Bathtub

"He knew her through and through, in all the intricate labyrinth of her lonely heart, better far than she knew herself."

Hindsfeet on High Places, Hannah Hurnard

The PI I hired had been working on his own investigation of the missing person I'd found. He talked with many of her family members.

He also called the local police and was instrumental in setting up a meeting for me. I met with them several times over the ensuing years. I had originally called the county police, but jurisdiction belonged to the city, because that was where the murder occurred. So, jurisdiction was changed, and a file opened there. The years had beaten me up pretty good, so I left the case in the hands of the detectives. Well, kind of.

Grizzly flashbacks from the murder continued to haunt me. One night, I woke and felt the presence of the woman I had met that sunny day in June take my hand. Another time, I had a dream that my family was at the drive in, Dad at the wheel, my brother and I sitting next to him. The murdered woman was lying on the floorboards, and we were resting our feet on her body. Her clothes still looked good, but her throat and hair were bloodied and disheveled. We continued to watch the movie like nothing was wrong. I was aware she was beneath our feet, but the movie wore on. When it ended, everyone got out of the car, and I was standing beside it.

Dad threw me the keys and said, "We'll meet you at home."

I was going to have to get back in that car alone, with her dead body, and drive home. I woke up and couldn't breathe. It took me about four hours to calm myself, after I called a friend to come over and sit with me because I was just so scared.

Soon after this, I made an appointment to go see Sara. I didn't stay in therapy consistently. I'd try, but it took so much time, and kept the wound fresh, so, I'd try to go without it until I knew I needed a tune up. She had since moved her practice to a town an hour's drive away. She candidly told me that she had taken me as far as she could. "Jodie, you have huge guy issues. I want you to start seeing the man who was my mentor. He's in Portland. He can help you."

I didn't want to leave her but understood that he was better equipped for my next journey. So, I started then with Foster. Over the following years, Foster would explain to me many things. He explained what sensory memories are and how they can intrude in unexpected ways: through panic attacks or insomnia, through dreams and artwork, through seemingly inexplicable compulsions, chaotic nightmares, or bodily pain and sensations. I was having many of these and his explanations helped me not fear. This murdered woman was not hunting me, my memories were.

My family began to talk about the murder amongst themselves. One night, my nephew and his wife came to see me. They told me a story they had kept to themselves over the years, because it was so outlandish and most likely would not be believed. They were telling me now, because, after learning of the murder, it began to make sense to them.

On the compound my parents maintained they had a manufactured home for rent. My nephew and his ex-wife rented it many years ago. Strange happenings occurred on that property and their family did not escape that. My nephew's ex-wife, Tiffany, is a bold, beautiful woman. She has a way about herself that seeks out the hidden. No ordinary discussions or circumstances would bind her to deny the things she witnessed. She left that property believing there was a women's body buried there. She thought she was buried under the trailer they were living in.

She told me about the day they left the property. She got up with her first-born son who was an infant at the time. She gave him a bath and returned to her bedroom. She was playing with her son and bouncing him on the bed. The covers shifted and a pile of maggots were exposed. She had just gotten up and the maggots were not there. She said there were so many piles of maggots they were falling off the side of the bed. They packed up everything immediately and moved out that day. I remembered Mom telling me how upset she was that the "kids" just up and left – no explanation, nothing. Now I understood that they simply could not stay. There was resident evil on my dad's property.

Then, on another afternoon, my nephew and niece were over visiting. They had lived on my parents' property for several years as small children. There were forty acres in the Steele estate, and my other siblings all placed homes on the five acres they were given. I never took my inheritance. It was dripping in blood and came with a price tag of silence. Anyway, my brother brought his family to the mountain. I told him then it was a bad idea, but he probably felt it was the easiest way to have a home.

The kids chatted with me a lot in those days. One day, their mother called me and said, "Jodie, can you come over and talk with the kids? Your brother told them that you said Papa murdered someone."

I went right over. I told the kids I was sorry that their dad had told them this. They were far too young, but now that they had been told, I wasn't going to lie to them. I explained to them that Papa had killed a woman but included no other details.

The kids then lit up like an over decorated Christmas tree with their own stories of their time on the mountain. They explained how they would see a hooded figure running from one room to the next in their home on the mountain. They no longer lived there but could easily recall the fear of it all.

Then, my nephew said, "Aunt Jodie, I saw a woman with blonde hair walking out of the woods one night. How was she killed, Aunt Jodie? This lady had her throat slit."

I could not believe what he was saying. This was very early on, and I hadn't spoken the details of the murder to anyone, except the police and my mother. He said it was not a dream, that he was playing outside and saw her walk out of the woods. I am not a spiritualist, nor am I schooled in what happens to a soul after it leaves the body, but there are some phenomena that leave a voice behind after the event of the crime. I was learning that through these stories of those left on the land she was buried on. I tend to believe that it's God way of righting a wrong. It seems unfair, and not very plausible, that a human spirit would roam the earth until it found justice. However, I believed the stories and was intrigued.

Then, my niece said, "Hey, Josh, remember that time I told you about when the teacup in my room turned in the head of a blonde lady?"

Those poor babies had seen evidence of horrible betrayal. Was it because they lived on the property where her body had been thrown? I'll never know the why and I don't need to.

These years, I spent more and more time trying to gain self-understanding and heal those desolate areas within me. With the police on the case, I had more time available and there was nothing else I could do but work on solidifying the experiences in my soul. I had spent years before going through the sexual-abuse memories and had a solid understanding that the fastest way to incorporate them was to walk through them –which included talking through, processing, and integrating the memories.

Unfortunately, just because I knew this, didn't mean I always followed through. I would drag out times between visits to Foster. Sometimes it would be a year or more before I would reschedule. It just felt like too much sometimes. I wanted to smell the sunshine and taste the rain. Be free like other people who haven't been through my experiences.

Maybe that added time to my healing process, maybe it didn't. I cannot redo that now and don't know if I even would. It was fast enough for the standards of what my being could tolerate.

I went on a *Fight for the Cure* walk-a-thon early one morning. Afterward, a few of us stopped for breakfast. I came home that afternoon and felt uneasy. I tried to go upstairs to lie down to take a nap. She was standing there. The dead lady. In my room. She looked at me with a dull stillness. What the fuck was going on?

I told her that she needed to go talk to Dad or Craig. They had murdered her, I had not.

And then she was gone.

When I'd have the courage to talk with my counselor about these things, he'd remind me that this wasn't her *spirit* in my room, but rather just a recall or a flashback. It felt like her spirit to me.

This was a bit of a recurrence in those days. I could be trying to get away for some R & R on a weekend beach trip, and while on the porch enjoying some quiet time, I'd see her coming out of the woods, walking up to me. I ran inside because it scared the shit out of me. When I talked with Foster, he'd explain it again for me. He'd ask me to think about where I had seen her – like she was being portrayed in the image. I was always surprised. Each time I could say, "Oh, you know when you ask me like that, that was when she was on the sidewalk walking toward me." There was always a memory that I could place with these strange recalls. Like I say, a good counselor can change your life.

In July of 2008, my life was completely torn up with the discovery of the murder, coupled with life in general. My legal career was still going, and my workdays were so difficult. My mind always trying to retrace more of my past, I held on minimally to everything else. I couldn't wait for the workday to end and go to happy hour and find some relief from it all.

During these years, my mother maintained an occupation closer to me. The pretend helper to guide me as much as she could, away from the whole disclosure of our ugly past. It confused me but I wanted to hope she was there with good intentions.

Brit and I decided on a road trip to see Brooke, who lived in Utah with her husband and two small children. I was beyond excited to go spend time with the loves of my life -- my children and grandchildren. This also bought me some time away from the realities of my life.

The night before I left, I walked into my home office, opened the drawer that housed my entire discovery of the murder case, looked at it intently and decided. I was done. I was done with this whole mess, and I didn't care if she came out of the ground; I didn't care if it was the truth, or I'd made it all up; I simply wanted to be done and walk away. I closed the drawer hard, trying to punctuate my thoughts, and firmly stated, "I'm done. I'm closing this chapter of my life. I am going to walk away. This has taken enough from me and my children and I'm going back to life – without *it*."

We began our road trip, excited for adventure ahead. About half-way there, we looked for somewhere to stay. I always tried to ensure that anywhere we stayed would not be like the motel where the murder occurred. We pulled off the interstate and I was apprehensive as our options were not good. But we found one.

We got out of the car, grabbed our stuff, and walked up to the room. The curtains were open in the room preceding ours. Holy shit. That room was set up just like the room at Riverside Motel. I said nothing to my daughter and tried to do the mind-over-matter thing. I'd be fine, I promised myself.

When Brit opened the door to the room, I couldn't get myself to walk through the door. Fear gripped my legs and told me to run.

My daughter, who was in her early twenties at the time, said, "Mom – I think it would be good for you to go into the room."

My skin crawled as we stepped over the threshold. A time warp was happening – I could feel it. The air was foggy with dissociation setting in. The walls were the dingy white from '68 and I could hear the sounds of that fateful morning. I was back – it was June 8, 1968.

I couldn't breathe. I couldn't think. I needed to get out of there, but my daughter was by my side, and I needed to be strong. Oh, God, help me. Brit opened a bottle of wine and I tried to drink some, hoping it will bring some relief, but nothing could release this gripping anxiety that was surging through my body.

Brit asked if I was okay.

I said, "If we're going to stay in this room, we have to take the bedspread off the bed and put it over there, against the wall." This was nuts. Was I losing my mind? But I would have lost my mind if I hadn't removed that bedspread.

She agreed and I asked her to move her feet off the bed so I could take it off, fold it up, and place it on the floor. What the hell did I need to fold the bastard up for? This was insane but I simply had to spring into action. My past was guiding my movements.

This strange reoccurrence of events was happening in me. I was terrified, to say the least. I sat back down, thinking that would satisfy this strange urge inside of me. We'd be okay now that the bedspread was off the bed.

Then, it came to me as soon as I sat down. I said, "Sis, they put her in the bathtub. We've got to pick that bedspread up and put it in the bathtub."

It was all so bizarre. I must tell you that I had to follow through with these actions. It was like something inside of me was directing everything.

I picked it up and placed it into the tub. I walked out and sat down. There was not a moment that I wasn't crying, acting odd, and feeling absolutely possessed with emotion and confusion, yet utter clarity about what had happened that day in '68.

With fog surrounding my daughter's face, I stopped and focused on her. She wanted to hide her face from me but did not. Pain etched the corners of her mouth into a slight smile. She was almost frozen with fear but held determination for me. I wrapped my arms around her, holding back the guilt of bringing her into this room with me.

We were both crying now. I told her we had to get out of here. I could not stay in that room another minute.

We packed up but I needed to go to the bathroom before we left. I tried to walk into the bathroom, but fear of this dead woman greeting me blocked my ability to move. I peed in the sink, in the area next to the bathroom, as awful as that was. It felt like the dead woman was there. Her spirit standing right beside me. I couldn't get out of that room fast enough.

I asked Brit to drive. I had grabbed the wine we opened, you can be sure of that, and was trying to put it down as fast as I could. I needed these surging feelings to go away, and alcohol could at least get me breathing normally again. And then, the strangest feeling came over me.

I felt the presence of that little girl, small Jodie, who'd just watched the murder. I turned my face away from my own daughter, in embarrassment of what had just happened. I was simply overwhelmed. With my face toward the window, I allowed my mind to go over the words I was hearing. The only thing I could hear over and over in my mind was, "Don't tell. You can't talk about this. Don't tell anybody." I let my mouth form the words, without any voice, hoping this would get it out of me, tears rushing down my face for miles.

We drove through the night, arriving in Utah the next morning. So much of me could not be present with my girls or my beautiful grandchildren. For the duration of the trip, I was in the shock wave of last night's discovery and the fog of PTSD. My decision to close the case and walk away wasn't a decision I really had control over. This was an experience I wouldn't be able to put back in a categorized drawer and close shut.

Soon after I returned home, I contacted the same PI via email. The subject line – *Getting Back in Touch About the 1968 Murder.*

Hi Chris! It's been a while since we've talked. I'm sure I don't have to say much for you to remember who I am. Jodie White, murder at Riverside Inn in 1968. This case was assigned to a Vancouver Police Detective....about a year ago. I've heard nothing from him. I've sent a few emails, with no response. This may be normal, but unfortunately, I'd like to have this resolved and the woman buried appropriately. With that said, I'm not sure what I can do. You had mentioned to me that I should, with your help, talk with Craig...the other man that was in the room with me and my father. Maybe I should.

Last week I stopped on a road trip and rented a room. I walked into a room that was almost identical to the room we had all been in 1968. I was terrorized with memory. As you can imagine, I only made it in that room about two painstaking hours. So, I guess it was an expensive counseling session. The intriguing part   I had just put the file away the night before and said I was done. I wasn't going to look at it again. I don't know how these passings of the slain work, but it seems she wants peace...or God wants me to continue until it's finished. I don't truly know. But, I want rest. I need rest from this tortuous hideous occurrence.

I don't have a lot of extra money. I was engaged, relocated, it didn't work (imagine, if you will, I have tremendous trust issues)...it cost me about $10,000 to move back. I am still willing to pay you, but I'd like to do what I can to reduce the cost somewhat.

Where would you go from here? Do I patiently wait for

*the overworked Vancouver Police Dept. to respond? Or do I
move forward with your help.*

Thank you, Chris. I'll wait for your reply.

Jodie

Trying to find relaxation, I ran a hot bath – my go to. This night as I submerged my head under the water, I had an instant recall of the woman before she was murdered. She sat next to me on the floor, her legs tucked beside her. She opened her purse for me, offering the contents as a source of play. I rushed out of the water gasping for air. Then I sobbed. I had just remembered another piece of the puzzle.

Sixteen

This Ones for You, Dad

"No trauma has discrete edges. Trauma bleeds. Out of
wounds and across boundaries."
-- Leslie Jamison

I missed my family so much. I hadn't done anything wrong but fight
our father for the truth. I also had done my part to bring protection
and safety to the children who were left behind me in this great line
of destruction. The first grandchild born into the family, a boy, was
like a son to me. I stayed close to him and his children until the day he
walked out my front door and never returned. My brother's children
are beautiful gifts that I purposefully stayed close to until they grew
and could make choices for themselves. There were other nephews and
nieces I could not be close to because of the denial of their parents.

I knew one thing always -- I had to keep with the truth of what
I knew so they would have at least the chance to see a different way,
to hear a different story. A story that rung with the sound of clarity
and truth. A chance to avoid being touched sexually or live out a life of
denial like the rest of them. But, because I wouldn't be quiet about my
family stuff, I was not welcome. Despite all of this, I still had a longing
to belong somewhere amongst them. I found that if I tried to stay close
to those who had been singed by the fire my parents breathed on us

year after year, their struggle to be different wasn't present. They were more like my parents than I wanted to believe. The abuse wasn't dead. I just couldn't stay close to them, and they clearly did not want to be close to my truth either.

I felt punished for defending the pursuit I found myself committed to. Why didn't they understand that I fought on their behalf, too? Their judgment of me was so difficult to live with that during the Christmas of '08, I typed these words, printed them, folded it up, and put it in my wallet. This was my reminder that I had to go o

No more proving .... Cussing....trying to be treated fair. It is what it is. No more. No less. Love me if you will....reject me if you will. I'll not try to be someone I am not. I do not have to be accepted by you to make it in this life. Unfortunate? Maybe – maybe not. I'm not sure I want to know who you are any more than I do.

I took that note out often through the next many years and it did help. I changed my expectation that I would be loved by any of them.

By now, I'd been engaged in combat with my family for the last twenty years. It started when my children were babies and my confrontation about all the sexual abuse in our childhood. Now, it was the memory of the murder. I had reached a pinnacle of anger with it all. I found this email five years after I wrote it, in my email's sent items. I was taken aback by the contents. I was also proud of myself for sending it. I always tried to take the most non-angry approach, but anger is not always a bad thing. I could have changed some of the foul language but I didn't. This is exactly how I sent it to my father, two days after Christmas in 2008. Okay, so that note I kept in my wallet said no more cussing. Well, that didn't happen, but my expectations did change.

The email's subject was "This one is for Stan." And it began:

Before you die you mother fucker...I'd like to tell you just what a piece of shit you are. I have held my tongue, said it nice, fuck that. I'm so angry at you I could kill you myself. I am sick of this pain. How do you live with yourself?

I remember it all Dad...do you? The white shirt your victim was wearing...her skirt. Do you remember how you held her down with the back of her neck while you used your free hand to get her vagina ready for you? I remember...I remember it all. You sick sick mother fucker. I hope you burn in hell for what you did to her. I do.

And Craig...was he your lover or just another sick bastard that got your dick hard? How do you live with your secrets? You killed a woman and sleep at night. With her right down the hill from you...what the fuck! I am so angry at you. You have taken so so much and you still have breath. Where is the fairness is any of that...you deserve to be damned to hell. Which...by the way. is exactly where you're going.

The bible says ...father....if you CONFESS your sin. he is willing and able to forgive it. You sick fucker you haven't confessed anything. And before you die I wanted to tell you exactly what kind of person I think you are. You are miserable excuse a waste of fucking air. I wish I could watch as someone sliced your throat! Scripture Dad...remember. An eye for an eye so a slit throat for a slit throat.

Do you remember the smell of her blood. Unfortunately I fuckin do. The stench of death before I was hardly even alive. You killed a large piece of me. And then expected me to just be good. no acting out or you'd hurt me again. God...I am so tired of being quiet for you!!!!!!!!!!!!!! You deserve hell. I hope you go there.

I was a good daughter...you demanded that. Fuck you Dad!!!!!!!!!!!!!!!!!!!!!!!!!!!!!!!!! You deserve nothing from me. and nothing is what you get. Nothing.

Does it go through your mind how you wrapped her in the bedspread and put her in the trunk of your car? Even Craig cried...but you fuck no. You don't feel. Maybe you can feel this..FUCK YOU! I hate you   I don't have one ounce of love for you. no one should/ Good thing there is a god who may love you...cuz there aint many others that do. For good reason....

And go ahead and use this against me. What the fuck else can you take from me....what Dad. Show Cinnamon...show Claude I don't give a fuck! There is nothing else you can take cuz you're too fuckin sick to hurt me anymore. or I'm sure you'd be at my door.

I hope her murder is broadcast from the rooftops Dad another biblical line. If I can do anything about that I plan to!

Rot in hell

My mother had given me a picture of a drawing I had made for Dad in November 1968, only five months after the murder. Dad wrote above the picture, "drawn by Jodie Lynn age 4 for her Dad 11/24/68." He didn't even spell my name right. Then, very crudely sketched, was a stick figure; a head, two legs, two feet, and one very large stick penis drawn in just the right place. After the image, Dad wrote "Daddy Stan Steele."

I took it to Foster and sent the picture to the police (that's why the sheriff's office stamp appears on the picture). I heard they had several independent professionals look at it and their consensus was that "this child" had been sexually abused. Like Foster told me, "If your dad had any sense to know what you were depicting, he would have never kept it." Dad wasn't always the best at seeing all angles, but he did get away with murder. He kept it as evidence of my unconditional love for him; not knowing it had captured a piece of who he was. Here's that picture:

drawn by Jodie Lynn age 4 for her dad
11/24/68

Daddy Stan Steele

000013

October 2009, I stopped drinking for a while and started journaling. One of my entries reads, "I'm sitting in the airport – heading to San Francisco to board a cruise ship to Mexico. Twenty days clean and sober TODAY! It's like a scientific experiment." And, indeed, sobriety was an experiment. It wasn't what healed me.

Maybe the desire that my life could help someone else was a motivating factor for me to continue. It was a choice I had to make each day. Some days I choose to ignore reality and simply look the other way. I had to sometimes, or I wouldn't have made it through the tiresome journey that the road to discovery of the past takes.

Another entry reads:

Names, faces, men and boys. Shit – what is it they can bring? More pain? Agony? Desire is what they move within me. And, yet, I believe each and every time they will elude any form of fulfillment. I want to try. I want to believe. I want to be vulnerable. But how? Why? No love in. No love out. This is not good. So, I'm going to try. Not today, but tomorrow.

Much of the wasteland that had been left in my life was the inability to have a meaningful relationship with men. My abusive 18-year marriage, coupled with all the devastation my father left, kept me within that familiar prison of being alone. It was the only safe place.

And the second to the last entry reads:

"Day 54: Holy fuck! This sobriety is TOUGH! Pain – overwhelming at times. Loss of my family. Loss of my children's innocence at the hand of their father. Loss of protection. Well, loss of protection for myself is something I've not had to lose so just an overwhelming feeling of being alone – without someone to watch over me.

Where was and is my mother. I hate her at times -- a lot of the time. I'd like to beat her so she could feel my pain. And, yet – I don't want to hurt her. She's fucking frail, weak! What a joke.

It takes strength to deny and stay with fucked up men! So, she's got strength. She just uses it wrong.

I started drinking again after only three months. It's about the journey and trying to take a few steps forward. I went easy on myself and realized I wasn't perfect, either.

I continued to move forward in whatever form that looked like. Foster suggested that I tell my father I had gone to the police. Before this time, Dad didn't know I had an open police investigation. Out of respect, I wrote to Zapata in April of 2009:

Subject: 1968 -- James Steele

Good morning,

I hope the day finds you well and rested. In the deepest respect possible, I wanted to tell you that I plan to go speak with my father. I feel that the closure this will bring to my life is important, maybe one of the most necessary things I could do to complete this outstanding ward of secrecy between my father and me.

You asked me in the past not to say anything to him about going to the police. I've honored that request. However, in speaking with my counselor (that I see from time to time for tune-ups) he felt strongly that I should talk with my dad about my accomplishments, one of which is telling you all about his crime. I told my counselor you'd requested that I not speak with him due to the element of surprise. His advice to me was that I'm in a state of limbo, and for closure in my life regarding this time, i needed to talk with my dad about it.

I had to agree. It rang very true to my soul. So, I wanted to give you notice so you could have time if you needed it. On Saturday, May 2, 2009, I'm going to go see my father and talk with him about all of this. I need to before he passes, which is probably not far away. I'm told by my mother that daily he takes almost lethal doses of medication, and drinks heavily. I need to find peace before he passes.

Thank you so much for all of your labor and sincerity. If the case cannot be solved before his death, I still must pursue my own needs in its completion. I pray that after his passing we can simply excavate the dump site and return her remains to her family.

Again, thank you for everything.
Jodie

His response came nineteen days later:

I apologize for the slow response. I agree that your mental health is of
greater importance and in the end it shouldn't have a negative impact on
what I'm doing. I'll be interested to hear about the outcome of your contact,
so please keep me in mind.

I did go see my dad, but, honestly, I cannot recall exactly how this visit went. It's safe to assume nothing *earth moving* happened.

December 2010, my mom called me and said that Dad would be going on hospice, and he would only have hours or days to live. She added that if I wanted one last visit with him, I'd better get to the house as soon as I could.

Fear that this would be my last shot of rejection from him was almost more than I could bear. I was terrified, but I went.

Seventeen

Murder | A Flip Book

> "You're breaking generational curses. That's why this
> doesn't come easy for you. You're who your bloodline has
> been waiting for."
> — Unknown

Foster and I continued our work through the years, and I began to piece the story together. As if writing one of those small books where you put together a different picture, slightly different than the last, and then thumb through it to make an entire story. That's exactly what I did with my memories.

One evening in my old Craftsman home, I grabbed a bottle of wine and began the journey of putting it all together -- everything my body and mind had discovered to this point. I brought it to Foster in our next appointment and read through it with him.

He said, "Jodie, that's remarkable what you've just done. It's very smart of you to put it all together in the timeline as it happened."

After forty painstaking years, this is the sequential happenings of the day we murdered.

The month was June of '68. I was three, but not for long. I'd turn four the following month. My father and I were driving down a lonely, local interstate highway in a four-door sedan. The car was a silvery blue, with black interior. I learned later from my mother that this was my grandmother's car but that is not part of my memory. Dad was preoccupied, but he was enjoying the lit cigarette pinched between his fingers.

It was a sunny day, and I was happy to be with him. He was my world. It didn't matter what he did. He was the power. He took a left off the highway and drove slowly up to an unfamiliar building. He took me out of the car and sat me in a white plastic chair, my little legs extending beyond my summer dress. He disappeared. I looked around, taking in my environment. It seemed like something I had learned how to do, to try and keep myself alert, away from harm. Across the highway was a hill topped with railroad tracks. My brother's toy train made me wonder what a real train flying past might sound like. I was lost in this moment of childish wonder, until I felt a woman with soft, small hands reach out and take my own, ripping me from my thoughts. This moment is one I will guard for eternity.

She was a blonde woman, dainty, pretty, and petite. She tried to speak with me, but my father interrupted abruptly, grabbed my arm, and moved me away from her. I remember wanting her to stay. I pranced on my tip toes to keep up with Dad as he dragged me down the concrete sidewalk past the windows and doors. He was angry and I couldn't afford any indifference to his need, only compliance. He opened a door to a room with no sunlight. He picked me up by one arm, swatted me, and sternly told me to stay put.

I'd never been in a motel room. My unexperienced mind reasoned that this place was a bunch of bedrooms. I explored it with innocence and fear. I came to rest against the bed for a second, and ran my fingers across the scraggy, rough bedspread. It felt fake. We didn't have anything like this at home. The walls had no color. There was a window, but the curtains were closed, exposing none of the outside world. Next to it, a television stand, with a junky old TV that wasn't turned on. Beside the bed was a table with a lamp resting on it. The room was dark because the curtains were closed but the lamp threw a dim light. Behind a small wall I could see a doorway but hadn't the desire to look there. Someone could be hiding around the corner like the time the boy was hiding in the basement at my babysitter's house.

I moved myself backward as close to the wall as I could get. From that position, I could see both doors. I believed and had learned that there was a form of protection in being alert, so I continued to watch vigilantly and stay on guard. I was ready to wait in that room with the offensive dense and musky smell.

The door burst open. I was so happy someone was joining me. In walked my dad, Craig, and the woman from outside. They poured some drinks and continued chatting. This was going to be a party. I knew what parties were because my parents often had them in our home. My fear started to release -- this was something I was familiar with – but I kept my eye on Craig. If Craig and Dad were together, nothing good would come of it. Me and my siblings had been part of many of their hedonistic sexual campaigns before.

Craig was a man of great stature, he towered over me as a child like a filthy lumberjack. His words were few. He reminded me of the character, Chief Bromden, in the movie, *One Flew over the Cuckoo's Nest*. The great big Indian whose first words in the script were: "Juicy Fruit." Craig visited our house often in those days. I always knew he was into my father on a much deeper level than just as a drinking buddy. He'd do just about anything for him, and he did. He loved my father and was his right-hand man.

On Delaware Lane, they were inseparable. Craig worked at a local plant called Alcoa. He sometimes had his blue work coveralls on after a shift when he came over to the house. When Craig visited our home, he always had some form of candy with him. I tried to remember him only for his candy, trying to escape the turpitude that dwelled within him. How loving children are. For a mere mint, they'll send a smile your way, knowing all the while who you truly are. I can't tell you much more about who Craig was outside of the ugliness -- a child molester. Dad let him join in the predator fun charades of the incestuous home he ran. Seemed he and Dad pretty much drove, drank, and studied together. They studied humans who were weak – or at least weaker than they were. Children are the most vulnerable, so we didn't require much study.

After some time, the lady sat on the carpet next to me. She leaned her head toward mine and spoke softly. It felt like a signal from her that I would be okay. She tucked her bare feet along the left side of her body and brought her face close to mine. She talked for a moment, but saw I was apprehensive. My father had just warned me not to talk to her but in kindness, she pushed through, opened her purse, and offered some playful exchange with me. I eagerly explored its contents with her. They all continued drinking and having a good time. I was having a good time too: people around my father meant he couldn't be himself -- bad.

Then, the cold air of my father's temper stirred. He started to pace. His fear of losing control was showing. He wanted something that he did not yet have. He seemed preoccupied by the time elapsing and felt his opportunistic window was closing.

Didn't everyone see the transformation happening? We needed to run and hide, but no one moved. I wanted to, but my natural reaction had been long ago beaten out of me. The best position would be to remain glued to the wall and just keep watching.

With the stage now set and the curtain drawn, Dad began his show. The credulous nature of a three-year-old cannot now bring the details I would like to. These moments returned to me in snapshots, not fully animated, but frozen. Piece by grueling piece, through the years, they returned to me. As in my reoccurring dream, I now saw the first freeze frame. The woman is being forced to lie on the bed, her stomach to the mattress. Dad is, of course, orchestrating the entire event. He's holding her down forcefully, his right hand tightly around the back of her neck -- her hair tangled in his grip. I knew that hand was strong and forceful.

She wore a darling cotton skirt with a tucked-in white, short-sleeved blouse, the kind of blouse that buttons all the way down the front. He used his free hand to push up her skirt, and then navigate toward his targeted desire. I was aware of his goal. When he'd finished raping her, she struggled free from him and moved herself up onto the bed.

As she scooted, she screamed at him. Her words engulfed the air with terror. Struck by her tenacity to fight back, I'd never seen this in a woman before. She could form her words so well that it was casting a shadow of doubt on my father. How would he stop her? I could sense his fear.

She continued to yell, "You're going to pay for this!" Secretly, I loved it, although I knew it would be her who paid the price in that room. Dad could not allow another outcome. I remained immobilized against the coarsely painted, harsh wall. The wall was cold and impersonal. I needed something -- someone to hold me. Something soft I could rely on.

If I could have warned her, I would've given it a valiant effort, even though I was too small to speak and too tiny to fight. "Run," I would have said. "Hide, beneath the first rock you find. It would be better than the fate for you here. Run! I'll stay." I had to. I was betrothed upon my birth. She would never hear any words from me, not one. Given just one privilege in that room, I would have told her to go! To keep her damn mouth shut. She shouldn't be taunting them with her voice. It's still frightening to reexamine the walls of that room through words. A story I was never supposed to expose for fear my fate would match hers.

Act II began with her continued struggle. Now on her feet she aimed her battle at the man who had just raped her. She blocked Craig. Behind him, a shadow from the dimly lit lamp cast despair onto the scene.

Dad took his position directly in front of her, now with a new determination. I felt the cold in his heart seep through the air. His fear was turning to rage, and he was giving into it. He'd stop at nothing but her silence. Some forty years later, I would learn from him that he felt he had no other choice. Well, I may be adding that to his story because it makes it easier for me to digest.

I cannot regurgitate her words to you, but I knew her language was threatening to him. She was planning to hold him accountable for what he'd just done.

At some point my mind skipped to the next slide in the projector and Craig took her arms from behind, holding them down firmly to her side, now in front of the lamp she was trapped, again. Without a dribble of compassion, my father swings at her once.

My heartbeat drummed away most of the disturbing noises that flashed all around me. In my father's hand was the blade of death. I knew it was the knife that would grip the confusion of that place and shut it all down. Dad was known for keeping his Southern hospitality strapped to his belt. In one moment, everything was hushed to an eerie silence.

I have been asked by counselors and others if I thought I was going to die that day, too. I can emphatically say, "No, not that day. If I told, yes. If I kept quiet like any good accomplice knows, I wouldn't be in line to be murdered. I could keep my life, as they kept theirs, with just the sacrifice of silence. I was their good friend. Secrets of this magnitude build bonds that are strong and cannot tolerate betrayal. So, no I wasn't scared I'd have my throat slit. No."

They sprang into action as if they knew exactly what to do next. Dad bent down and grabbed her by the ankles and carelessly laid her to rest on the floor. Oddly, it did seem like rest for her now. I was too inexperienced to know she was dead. I could only see her bare feet protruding from the end of the bed, my gaze involuntarily frozen on them. These sights etched a design in my soul that would follow me through life, beckoning my return.

Dad then walked through the secondary doorway, which I now recognized to be the sound of a bathroom. I could hear the water running and I surmised he was washing off his hands and cleaning his prized metal possession. He was proud of the courage that small sword gave him. When he rejoined us, they picked up her still body and laid it back on the bed. They wrapped her slight frame in the scruffy old bedspread. Of course, he would take away someone who had been nice to me. I wanted her with me, oh, how I wanted her beside me now. They couldn't just wrap her up and throw her away, could they? They carefully picked up the package like a tightly wrapped salmon and placed it in the bathtub. It would take another forty years for me to have any recollection of the time they spent cleaning the mattress and the room.

The front door to this tomb was cracked open and cascading light from the outside world dripped onto the dingy carpet. Someone had backed up the car to the front door because this was not where Dad had originally parked it. The trunk on the car was agape and I watched in agony as they placed that bundle inside and closed her away to darkness. Dad told me to get in and opened the back door. He was preoccupied and didn't help me in. It was a challenge to climb my way into the backseat because I was so little. And then, knowing that once I arrived, I'd be seated in front of her. My body surged with anxiety that she would reach through and ask me to help her. I didn't want to be next to her. I had no help I could give her and the thought of it scared me to exhaustion.

Craig was in the front seat with Dad. He was crying and holding his face. "Why'd you do it? Stan, why'd you do it?"

There was no reply as my father continued in his silence.

We got onto the freeway where the first exit would have taken us home, but the car did not take that off-ramp, only continued down the highway. My heart sank. Someone needed to take me away from these two monsters. My tiny body plastered to the black vinyl seat, which was the only barrier between me and the woman it hid. My memory fades here, like someone turning the lamp down to go to sleep. I think, or I hope, I fell asleep. I'll never really know.

Reeling this unpredictable film forward, I was abruptly awakened to Dad and Craig getting out of the car. We had taken the long drive to the large piece of property my parents had just recently purchased. The trunk creaked open. With a blissful gaze, I saw them proceed past the car windows, with her in tow, knowing, for now, I could stay glued to the seat.

My next memory was at my paternal grandmother's house, standing next to my father as he hosed out the remaining blood in the temporary grave of his victim – that old Oldsmobile.

As the years delivered these freeze frames to me, I struggled through the memories with a staunch determination to invalidate them. This couldn't be real, none of it. As an adult, I pursued discounting these haunting returns with a vengeance.

With this new memory of the blood-soaked trunk of the Oldsmobile, I got in my car and drove to my grandmother's house, convinced that if the spigot was not in the exact location as I remembered it in the flashback that I would lock my trumped-up imagination away for the rest of my life. I drove to Shirley Avenue where my grandma's house was and the hose on the house was in the exact position I'd seen, just far enough to reach the street and filter away the evidence of this woman's existence. If I was going to regain even half of myself, this was further proof that I had to find the courage to remember it all. Even if it meant finding my own guilt.

The day continued until it became night. We had returned to the property, and they had been working off in the near distance for many hours. I was startled awake when the car door swung open, and Dad climbed into the back seat. We were in a different car now, one with only two doors. Dad had retrieved his own car after cleaning up Grandma's. My father began writhing his way into the backseat with me, quite drunk again and acting obnoxious and silly.

This is me and the gold car in 1968. I found this picture years after my memory returned at my parents' house.

Insert pic

What I learned later through the hospital records is that he was heading into a very serious diabetic coma. He dangled a necklace in my face, like a bizarre trophy. As his body collapsed on mine, I remember the heaviness of his head on my lap and the terror of his right hand shoved between my legs beneath my bottom, stirring fear of what would come next. That was truly all I knew – was what's next. They had finished their duties on the mountain that evening, and Dad began his descent into what would become the most severe diabetic coma of his life. At last, we headed home. I stared at Craig's silhouette as he drove, encouraged that I would be returning to our home soon. My mind fades away in that image with the bright thought that this day was finally ending.

We pulled into the driveway and my mother stood in the open door. I was so happy to get away from these two and needed my mom. It seemed very late and dark. The front door to our home on Delaware Lane was open, lights on, waiting for our return. Craig got out of the car and collected Dad out of my lap. My legs ached with an intensity I hadn't felt before. I wasn't sure how to make them work. Craig carried Dad into the house and laid him on the couch.

The next thing I remembered was standing in the living room, looking over at my father sprawled awkwardly on the sofa. He had an adoring fan club rallying to his aid. My mother hadn't been waiting for my return -- she'd been waiting for her husband's. I already knew this in my heart, but it saddened me, as I stood there alone. Had I eaten that day? No one cared to ask. What had I seen that day? No one's glance passed my way: their attention was on the man who had just taken a woman's life.

I felt so alone, once again.

My little world had been invaded by an act of destruction that I could never un-see. I felt a desperate need for someone to even look at me, for any kind of attention. If someone could have just held me, if even for a few seconds, those hours and the next hours of torture could have been eased. Truly, I would have settled for someone just talking to me. I was used to not receiving care, but I did need someone to help me. Maybe ask me what I needed.

No help came that night, or the next night – or the night after that one. As a statement of fact, no help has ever come into that moment but the help I've paid for through counselors and a great big God who never kept trying to find me.

With the commotion going on, I had no choice but to try to get myself to bed. With my legs on fire, like they'd been stung by hundreds of stinging nettles, they were betraying my efforts to get down the hall to my room. I gazed at my bedroom door, so far away. Another rush of panic surged through me. With my legs stuck to the floor, how would I ever make it to the safety of that room? I just wanted to sleep, but sleep would not find me. The only desire of those little limbs was to collapse, but it wasn't a luxury I could afford. I had to get down to my room, but how? The hallway may have been no more than twelve or fifteen feet long, but it might as well have been a football field. I recorded that passage intently. I see it even now as if it were before me. The overwhelming feeling of having to master it and my physical inability to do so boggled my simple mind.

I did make it. Did I drop to the floor and scoot my way down to my room? I'm not sure. Maybe in the gift of memory I decided that one should be tossed into eternal blackness. Why? The pain of being alone had already written its script on my heart and I still have a hard time ignoring it -- I didn't need the memory.

I sat against the wall perched on my bed now in darkness. Mangled shadows danced all around me, mocking any peace I could try to find. I could not close my eyes to the monstrous darkness. I just could not. I simply stared at the door. Possibly in anticipation of someone coming to find me, or, more likely, someone else coming to hurt me.

I spent many hours with these memories. I chatted with my therapist about why I continued to see that hallway. The scene wouldn't leave my mind's eye.

Finally, with full kindness and authority, Foster spoke these words that released that memory. "Jodie, you have to tell that little girl that no one is coming."

That broke my heart again, but it set that moment free for me. As I'd waited that night in 1968 for the morning light to peak its glorious head through my curtains, I learned I was still waiting. The only difference was that I could now let go of that hope.

No one was ever coming. But at last, I could rest.

Eighteen

Playing the Love Card

"The truth will set you free. But not until it is finished
with you,"
--David Foster Wallace, Infinite Jest

The monochrome color scheme of my office seemed to now scream complacency. I had tidy piles of to-dos here and there. A huge piece of me wanted to stay there in that lifeless air. I could lose myself in some dumb fucking tasks that didn't matter and ignore her phone call as she'd ignored my many pleas for help time and time again since I was tiny. But I needed to purge the words from my aching, parched soul that had plotted a course away from my dad many years before. Now, my feet that had run from him needed to walk toward him. One last time. One last time might be my final destiny of rejection from him, or I might find peace. I didn't care now which way it ended but now it was going to end.

I'd spent years refining my skill to compartmentalize and this would just be one final effort of that strategy. Strategy that he, the master, taught me by the way. If his final words were fuck you, then they were fuck you. I couldn't change that. But I had words I needed to say to him regardless of what he'd say back to me. My children deserved me to be strong too – hopefully gaining back a piece of their mother they'd never had. This was the final hour for me to plead my final cause to this man I had called *Daddy*.

I walked slowly to my car, dreading each step that brought me closer to his side. The last time I'd seen my father it didn't really go so well. After my verbal fishing expedition trying to recover any information about what made him such a bastard, he finally stood up, clenched his fists until they were white, came toward me, and sternly said, "Get the fuck out of my house!" I didn't want it to end that way again.

This wasn't going to be easy at all.

I pulled off the freeway and into a local bar where I knew the bartender. I ordered a double Cadillac margarita.

The bartender was dumbfounded at my early morning selection. She'd known me for a few years and was puzzled to see me so early. "Jodie! What's wrong?"

I told her that I'd just received a call from my mother and my father had only hours to live and that if I wanted a last chance to speak with him, I'd better make it today. I wasn't about to go over the horrific details in front of strangers. I wanted to scream from the top of my lungs, "What the fuck am I going to do! I can't do this. I cannot do this." My mind reassured me I didn't have the strength. I needed to get away from her, from reality! I picked up my double and walked to the back of the bar where there were poker machines. I'd lose myself here, if only for a moment. I slid a twenty into the money feeder and waited for my momentary fix.

I called two friends and asked them to accompany me to my father's castle, if they could. I had no family who'd stayed with me through the years because they just wanted me to shut the fuck up and I couldn't, so friends were my family now. I'd erected a plan for the day I received the call that Dad was leaving this planet. I had a long-standing relationship with this train-wreck boyfriend. We'd break up more than we were together, but we had each other's back in a revealing kind of way. That doesn't make sense, but neither do vast emotional caverns of hellish pain. We understood those dark places and shared a trauma bond. He and my friend, Sharon, were on their way to get me. That helped.

The way I normally drank was not going to cut through the fear, the trepidation of one final betrayal from my father. For this, I'd need straight booze. I hated straight booze but needed its calming effect on my muscles and nerves. Sharon kindly brought vodka to my house, as she knew the tortuous chore that lay ahead of me. I got a to-go cup and poured that liquid courage straight into the glass and didn't stop until it was half full. I was ready to start the thirty-minute drive up the mountain.

It was a bit overcast that day. Sharon drove and my ex-boyfriend followed. He was always the escape artist and needed his own car, but it was nice of him to go. It seemed surreal as the wheels turned close to what would be the final outcome between me and my father. So much of me didn't want to go and learn what he'd decide. Would he love me? Or would he extend his bitter denial?

Now, tonight, here I sat beside this sickly man for the last time.

(These are notes from the night I got home)

I walked in at 3:00 pm, Tuesday, December 7, 2010.

Dad and I began our discussion. I thought he'd send me out of the house in anger, but he didn't. The talk did not end until 8:30 pm.

"Dad, I'm here because hospice comes in tomorrow and they're going to start morphine. That means the end of your life. Before you go, I had to talk to you one more time."

He was in a distant place. It was like all the demons he listened to his entire life were finally silent and he was left alone with his choices. He made no recognition when I sat so I asked him who I was.

He said, "You're Karen."

He knew I was not my sister.

"Dad, you tell me who I am."

"You're Karen." He paused, "Well, you look like her." He hadn't even looked my way yet but may not have expected me.

Making sure we were on a truthful trek, I brought my face closer to his and said, "Fuck you, Dad, you tell me who I am."

He turned his head to me with one eye slightly cocked "You're Jodie Lynne Steele. You're my ornery one."

We could proceed now that he had given his full attention.

"I had to be mean to fight myself away from all that we'd been through," I answered. "If I wasn't your rebel daughter, I could not have grown stronger than you. You taught me a lot, Dad, and I used those rebel talents of yours to fight for good."

I tried to find the "R E B" tattoo on his arm. It took me a few tries to find it because the large, intimidating tattoo was now reduced to the size of a prune. I couldn't believe it. All was changing. The power he once had was gone.

I said, "I was there with you. I remember what we did."

He stared into an imaginary black hole in front of him and said, "I did terrible things to your grandma Baldwin." Then, a long pause. He said it again, "I did terrible, terrible things to her."

"Years ago, I emailed you and promised not to bring up Lynn's body until you were gone. Well, now that you're going, I'm going to try to bring her up and have her buried properly."

He said "I know you will" in a matter-of-fact tone.

"I've missed you through the years," I said remembering the times we'd played games, ate popcorn, and laughed together.

He softly replied, "I've missed you, too."

"God gave me to you, and you did a lot to hurt me, Dad."

He felt a bit threatened at that. His tone changed and he said frankly, "What do you want from me?"

"Dad, you've taken everything you could from me. I want nothing from you know. Your love is worthless. I'm here because I'm worried about your soul. I witnessed what you did."

He leaned further back into the couch, rested his hands on his knees, and said, "You wait a lifetime for a love like that."

There was a long pause of silence.

"I never got to know your kids...my grandkids."

"I couldn't allow them to be around you. I am sorry for that."

He said random things like, "You were the best looking one of my children."

What the fuck did that have to do with anything!

Wanting him to hear the cost of his actions, I continued, "Dad, I have been in such bad relationships with men. I haven't been able to love because of this bond between us. It's been really terrible for me."

We went in the other room to have a cigarette. The window there overlooks the field where the body rests. The field hadn't changed that much since I was a child. A plain view to the dumpsite. He could always keep an eye on it that way.

I pointed out the window and I told him, again, "I am going to have her body brought up and buried properly. I need to do whatever I can to make this right."

Quietly he said, "I know you will."

We moved back to the couch.

Questioning him, I asked, "Did you kill her to protect the family?"

He remained silent.

I asked him to look at me and he did. Looking into the possibility that he may not have always been evil, I said, "I don't think you showed up to be a horrible raping murderer. Were you hurt? You know, Dad, I've learned that God understands pain."

At some point, after a tough exchange of words, I asked him if he wanted me to leave now.

He replied, "No, I want your company."

"Dad, since we left that room alive and she did not, I have had tremendous guilt – you know, being alive."

His head moved slowly in my direction as he put his cigarette out.

"You didn't know I had guilt, did you?"

His gaze was now forward, he looked back into that invisible black hole in front of him. After several seconds of silence, he said, "I am so sorry."

Then, he moved slowly back to rest on the couch. Still staring ahead, he said very knowingly, "I am so sorry."

I chatted with him about the nightmares I'd have as a child – nightmares he gave me, but I'd run to him and lay my head on his chest for comfort. I told him I wanted to lay my head there one more time and cry. And I did. Years of pent-up anguish flowed onto his bare chest one last time. The hint of *Old Spice* long since gone.

"How do I let go?" I pleaded.

He sat up, and said, "I'm going to bed now." Under his breath he mumbled, "We shouldn't be talking about this."

I begged, "Please don't do that, Dad."

He didn't mention that again.

It was peaceful. I felt no rejection. I knew he was giving me permission to go live without his burden.

Looking down at his half-eaten leg, I said, "No one saw your pain did they, Dad? Your mother did not. I'm sorry about that. And that lady up in the kitchen, we both know she doesn't represent love," speaking of my mother. "Mom told me she thinks you have had peace through the years. I told her I don't believe you have." At times through the night my father would acknowledge the words I was speaking through a body language gesture – like turning toward me – this was one of those times.

Mom had come into the living room to lay him down. She was moving his legs up onto the couch and his privates almost showed. He tried to pull the covers over the exposed area. I told him not to worry about it, that it was nothing I hadn't seen before, and I smiled. Dad said nothing.

While Mom was laying him down, I told him, "Dad, I think Craig's going to jail."

He gave me the first surprising look of the evening and said, "What for? The child molestation?"

I replied, "No, Dad, for the murder. He held her arms."

Some kind of relief seemed to move over him, and he looked away.

I wanted him to know that his phony religion had not taken ahold of me.

"One night in my room on Delaware Lane I met Jesus, Dad. I couldn't see Him or really hear Him, but I knew He was there. He comforted me after all the torment. That's how I made it through. You know -- I didn't even know what His name was until I was eight. Remember that guy that came through that church we went to? His name was Gene Lewin. Gene Lewin's Jesus is the one you need."

He said, "I remember Gene Lewin."

I knelt in front of him and said, "Dad, I'll never see you again," and I cried.

He said, "You'll see me again."

"Why, Dad? Because of the Gene Lewin Jesus."

He said, "Yes."

I kissed him and left for the evening.

In the morning, I drove back to my parents' house. On the way, I received a call from Detective Peterson. I told him about the conversation with my father the night before. He said that I should put on a wire, go back to Dad, and see if I could get him to say it all again, only this time, record it. I told him I wouldn't do that. I was just too emotional. If I wore a wire, I wouldn't have been myself. My dad was a deceiver, I wasn't. I'd felt like I was betraying him to wear it, so I refused.

"Oh, and by the way, "Peterson said, "I'm on my way to Craig's house right now."

I told him to not go through with the interview right now. I was overwhelmed with emotion and the thought of Craig being interviewed while Dad lay dying was more than I could do.

When I arrived at Dad's house that morning, he had slipped into a coma. My daughter and I stayed for a few hours, but I didn't want us to be there when he passed. Additionally, my brother and sister were flying home. I had not seen either of them for years. Now was not the time for a confrontation. Although my mother told me she was on my side, she never really was, and I'd be an open target for them all.

I was sitting in my bedroom later that night. The Hank Williams song "Cold Cold Heart" played.

"Why can't I free your doubtful mind and melt your cold, cold heart."

Over and over the words ran through my mind. I could see an old record player in my mind's eye, spinning, while the words played through my heart and soul. After maybe the third time of the refrain, the phone rang.

I knew my father was gone.

My niece said, "Aunt Jodie, Papa just died."

At the same time, I had another call. Chris Peterson wanted to know his next step in the investigation. I told him I was on another call with my niece, that Dad had just died, and I wanted him to stop all work.

When I got off the phone, I wanted to hear all the words to the song. It felt as though my father sent it to me as he was dying. Maybe it was God, but I wanted to believe it was my dad signaling my final release.

I had an old Hank vinyl and put it on my record player. I listened over and over to the words.

A memory from your lonesome past keeps us so far apart
Why can't I free your doubtful mind and melt your cold, cold heart?
Another love before my time made your heart sad and blue
And so my heart is paying now for things I didn't do
In anger unkind words are said that make the teardrops start
Why can't I free your doubtful mind and melt your cold, cold heart?

I asked my father how I could be free. Did he leave these words with me to release me from the shackling of his memory?

My brother, sister, mom, and the rest of the family grieved together at my parents' house. I was home alone with my oldest daughter. The next day I called to just talk with my mom and my sister answered. I was crying and asked if I could talk to mom.

Karen said, "I'm not going to let you. You're going to make her cry."

For fuck's sake, we just lost our father – we should be crying. She finally let me talk to Mom. Mom explained that she would be over in the morning to talk. She was curious about the hours I spent with Dad.

She got to my house as she said she would, gave me an uncomfortable hug, and sat. "So, what did you and your dad talk about?"

"A lot, Mom. I was surprised with more secrets that he wanted to tell. I don't really want these secrets, but he gave them to me. Not sure what I do with them."

"Well, I'm sure he was just getting things off his chest," she replied as she dug for more.

"You know –he shared some stuff about Grandma. He said that he'd done terrible things to her. Then he paused awhile and said it again. What do you think he meant by terrible things?"

"Jodie, don't you ever tell anybody about that."

"Why, Mom? He's gone now. What do you think he meant by terrible things? Did he rape her?"

Mom tried to console me with, "No, they had an affair."

"An affair is not a terrible thing, Mom." She could not tell the truth of the situation, much like she lived her entire life. An affair with your mother is a terrible thing to most, but Dad was far from most. I knew Dad meant something much worse than intercourse.

The funeral was a joke. His grandsons were the only ones who said anything remotely close to the truth. One talked about having his first beer with Grandpa and the other said he remembers watching old war shows with him. Mom had designed the rest of the funeral to be a presentation of their bullshit. They represented him as a fine Christian man.

My brother got up and said, "I wouldn't know the Lord Jesus without his fine example."

WTF?

When the funeral was over, my nephews walked up to me and said, "What was that all about and who were they talking about?"

I am thankful that there were always remnants of truth that remained with the grandchildren.

December 9, 2011 – my journal reads:

"How can I love my siblings? They hate me, or at least pretend to. Let Jodie be the crazy one...we'll go stand over here and act like we're normal. Fuck them. They know it, and I know...and probably most people around them know, they are fucking liars. Every single one of them that says Dad was a decent man. Fuck you guys for that. How will that help you now? How did that help you then? I spent those last hours with Dad. I'm telling you now, it did not make one bit of difference to him that you lied for him. What it caused him to feel, was that you had no feelings....no love. no hate. Absolutely nothing. He knew it. I bet somewhere within yourselves you know it too.

Love would have told him the truth. That is what love does. Denial isn't embracing a person, it's ignoring them. So, you spent your adult lives ignoring your father, but hoped in the end he'd embrace you? Put a carrot seed in the ground, you'll grow a carrot. Doesn't matter   you cannot change a harvest after the seed has been planted. And, indeed, it is the harvest he deserved. He planted hate and received it from most. The sad thing is you continue to plant the same seeds he sowed. Sad, but somewhere I feel you deserve it too. You're doing the planting now. He's not!

A true survivor learns to tell her story. Out loud. Unashamed and in full control of the ownership of her destiny. That is the making of a survivor. Hate has no place at a survivor's table. Lies must be left at the door before you enter a survivor's house. Peace is their strongest comfort.

I don't think I've ever heard a story where a pedophile held full accountability for his actions. In cowardice, they hide. That is not surviving. I do not believe that my abusers hold any power that I don't possess.

Their ill-affected words do nothing but block their ability to live. They are imprisoned by the false walls and pretenses they build around their narrow lives. Do not stay by them long enough to believe their lies. Get down the road -- far are enough away that when they cast their deceitful nets (and they will) it can no longer entangle you. They hold no power that you do not possess yourself.

You know what I believe true survivors are? Those who find the ability to stand firmly in the truth. Not wavering in what their memories recall and listening steadfastly to what their bodies are telling them. Our stories live with us. Our mouths are what set us free. A true survivor loves. A true survivor lives.

About a month later, I sent the notes to Detective Zapata. Two detectives interviewed me about the six-hour conversation I had with my father. At the end of my interview, Zapata put his pencil down on his notebook.

Craeger said, "You can ask Zapata, but this sounds like a true confession. Men who do horrible crimes only confess or apologize to the least of their crimes. Oh, and by the way, Jodie, your dad could have done more to help you."

Maybe he could have but I knew one thing that they did not. The love potion's spell between me and my father had finally ended. That curse was over. I had played the love card between us, and I won that game.

Little did I know that much more of my past was going to be revealed. Dad indeed left a freedom in me. The exploration of our relationship was far from over.

Nineteen

Could It Be Madeline?

"A cheap Saturday night took you down. You died stupidly and harshly . . .I failed you as a talisman – so I stand now as your witness."
***My Dark Places*, James Ellroy**

After Dad's death, the police investigation didn't seem to be going anywhere.

I met with them one last time, but there wasn't funding, even if they wanted to help. The reality was that the murderer was also dead now. The last thing we were told is that they believed Madeline Babcock's remains had been found in Linn County, Oregon. If that were true, it would completely negate Madeline being the woman I remembered from 1968. We waited for the answer.

In the meantime, I talked with Foster about me spearheading an effort to get to know Madeline Babcock's sister. The police told me not to contact her, but I was running out of options and people were aging every day. I wanted to see if this sister had any information that would match anything I had.

Foster replied, "If the police aren't going to do any more, then certainly you have the right to continue."

I love how Foster taught me my rights. I did have rights, not just privileges.

I can never be certain if Madeline "Lynn" Babcock is the person buried in the sink hole that day, but you can be the judge and jury. I'm fine with that. My pursuit was not just mine alone, but for this woman I had met. I had to do all I could while there was still some sun light casting a ray of hope.

Madeline's sister, Pat Foy, had three websites in her honor that I had already found and scoured. Pat was now 75 years old and had spent a significant amount of time honoring her sister. Pat's roommate was Tipi, a beautiful parrot that she adored. She was now almost bedridden but continued her pursuit.

I saw that she had contacted *Webslueths*. This was new and I'd not yet explored it. To be a part of this website, you had to go through the verification process. My original post in July of 2012 on W*eblsueths*' thread for Madeline gave them the historical background information.

Soon after this email to *Websleuths*, my access was denied to their website. They did not believe my story and told Pat I was not credible. Before they removed me, Pat had a chance to respond to me. Here was our initial exchange:

> *"I am Madeline's blood sister please contact me and thank you from my heart for posting. I just want my sister buried with our family in Massachusetts. Please contact me when you an. Be my friend if possible. I miss my sister everyday. I understand her demise and how it could have happened. Please contact me. Patricia A Foy*

Pat and I could be two desperate women just consoling each other. That is a fact. We could also be two women who never gave up the hunt for justice. Piecing together what little we had, we found each other. Our facts lead us to each other. We could be wrong, but there were many things that did authenticate the possibility that my story matched her sister's disappearance.

Pat posted this two times. Then, I replied:

> *Hello, Pat. I'm Jodie. I don't know where to start. I hope desperately for all us that these two cases can end he suffering for everyone involved. How can I help you?*
>
> *I just don't know where to begin with you. I was a child when I met this kind blonde woman. She was with my father, James "Stan" Steele and his best friend in those days, Donald "Craig" Holbrook. I spent several hours with her before the end. I'll answer anything.*

Pat's response:

> *I recall talking to the Detective Peterson on the phone. I am 75 years young and I do recall talking to him. I was not sure of my cousin Claire's report of seeing Lynn in 1972. I think she tried to please my Mom who passed away in 1991.*
>
> . . .
>
> *I am glad you were with my sister, she loved children. Her temperament stems from being born with water on her brain. The first two years of her life were spent in a hospital. The doctors were able to relieve the fluid from her brain and she was a straight A student in school. I hope she died quickly and not suffered a long time. Can you email me at (she gave her email address).*

Then, my access was fully terminated to *Websleuths*. Don't think I have not had to remind myself time and time again that I am not bat shit crazy. Everyone else thought I was. My intention was not to bring more suffering to Pat, but to somehow vet through any remaining evidence we could piecemeal together. Pat and I exchanged email addresses and continued discussions. I was apprehensive to make any declaration that I knew for certainty that her sister was the one with us in '68. I was very careful not to build up false hopes for Pat or myself, but I had to try. I just had to.

During this time, a response to the DNA testing was received and Pat shared it with me. As posted on *Websleuth,* "I received a response from the University of North Texas. The DNA from the Jane Doe in Linn County, Oregon, was compared to the family reference samples provided from your family. Based on the DNA, this Jane Does has been excluded from being Madeline. The cases in NameUs will be updated to reflect this accurately as well." We now had confirmation that Madeline's remains were not matched to the remains found in Linn County.

With the confirmation that Madeline remained unidentified, I replied to Pat's email in July 2012, with much more detail. With some hope and courage renewed through this new information, I was willing to share more with Pat. I wrote:

> *I want to again remind you that I cannot be certain that the woman I spent time with on June 8, 1968, was your sister. I can tell you, however, that the woman I remember has a strong resemblance to Lyn. Added with the dates, the highway leading to Goldendale and other circumstances, it does lend towards a match.*
>
> *You've asked a few questions. First, yes, this is difficult for me.*
>
> *I was a very small child when the crime was committed. I'm told by professionals that these memories tend to be more accurate because the trauma behind them. In the years that followed, it has been proven that my memory was more accurate than that of the adults around me. For example, they told me that the night in question my father was admitted to the hospital during the day. The hospital records prove it was late in the evening. I knew that. They told me it was positively in 1969, the hospital records show 1968, in June. I told them exactly which two cars were used in the crime. My grandmother had one of the vehicles I described in '68, and my parents*

owned the other vehicle I described. I could go on with these details, but I'll stop there.

I just want you to know that the recollection of the woman I met in '68 can be trusted.

I cannot tell you how my father and Craig met this woman. I can only tell you where I come into the story. I was taken to the Riverside Inn motel by my Dad. He sat me in a white chair in front of the rooms and walked away. The woman and Craig were, obviously, already at the motel. Moments later I felt someone take my right hand. It was a pretty woman, with blonde hair and a kind smile. She asked me if I was Stan's daughter. I don't remember much else of the conversation.

Dad walked up and took me to a room down the walkway, and left me there. After some time, they all entered the room. It was the blonde woman, Dad, Craig and me. They were drinking and having a good time. The woman was compassionate towards me. I was sitting on the floor, against the wall, by the door. She came up and sat down next to me. Her legs were crossed to the left side and tucked a little behind her. Very lady like. She opened her purse and we spent time looking at the contents. I liked her. It seemed to matter to her that I was there. She was the only one in that room that seemed to notice me.

I don't remember any else until the woman is being sexually assaulted by my father. After the rape, she turned around and scooted up on the bed. She was screaming at my father. Telling him he was going to get it. She was going to tell on him. She yelled continuously and would not stop.

The next memory I have is her standing up next to the bed. Craig, the other man in the room, was standing behind her. He reached over and grabbed her arms, holding her so she couldn't get anywhere.

She didn't leave that room alive.

As for time where she talked to me, I was too small to remember the detail of any conversation with the woman. Just remember strongly that she was so kind to me. I wish I had more of her words that I remember, but I just don't.

My parents' had just purchased 20 acres in that time period. All three of us, with the body in the trunk, drove to the property. The day and detail is long, but she was buried in a large sinkhole on that property. I watched them work until dark covering up their crime.

I will do all I can as long as I am alive to bring up this body and have it buried with her family. I told my father on his deathbed that I would not stop until she was buried appropriately, with dignity -- for her family and ours. He told me "he knew I would."

And, I will. God willing.

All my care and concern...

Jodie

This was wild. I was talking to a missing woman's sister whom I had been monitoring for about seven years. Of course, I was quite nervous about it all. What if it wasn't her sister and I'd now misled this woman? Opened her heart for discouragement and let down? I felt a strong sense of protection over the situation so no one would be hurt.

Pat and I went back and forth. She asked me if the cars were still around. I had already gone down that avenue and the cars couldn't be discovered. Email after email we explored together. She did what she could to let me know she believed my story.

She wrote, "I know that was not easy for you to do. I want you to know that I respect your honesty. I believe it is Madeline. I only hope the police will look at all the facts. I broke my arm when I was two and a half years old. I still remember the kind doctor that fixed it for me. Jodie, you are a very brave woman and I appreciate you very much. We will figure out how to get this done. I am in a hospital bed here at home I am on a fixed income but, I will do all I am able to dig up the remains."

I'd read these emails and feared that I was wrong. Even after my father's deathbed apology, I couldn't be sure who the murdered woman was. Then it occurred to me, why did she think this was her sister?

As our exchanges continued, in July she forwarded me five pictures and asked me to pick the picture that most looked like the woman I met.

I replied, "I would have to say the two with arrows by them look most like what I remember. The morning I met her, her hair was down... just slightly past her shoulders. Did you ever know her to wear it that way? I'm guessing she stayed the night in the motel, and maybe hadn't done her hair that morning."

Pat answered with, "You picked the most recent pictures of Madeline Lyn, the last time I saw her she looked like that in May '68. It was Lyn and I believe you, Pat."

This still did not convince me that I had the right match. I was fairly certain, because I had described the woman who was with us before I received the hospital records, which gave us the date. A small dainty blonde. So, I felt good about the match, but not certain.

Pat asked for the Vancouver Police Department's information. She wanted to do her own follow up with them, and she did. After a conversation with the assigned detective, she told me, "I think the cost of the dig is of great concern and the memory of an almost four-year-old bothers him to make that call, you are right."

Each time my memories were scrutinized was brutal. If they had lived in my body, had lived through the minutes, hours, and days of body-felt recalls – the flashbacks, the nightmares, the torture -- they'd be certain, too.

In August, Pat sent me a picture of Madeline and her brother, Roy. It was taken in '66. Could this be the woman I met?

Pat wrote to the governor of our state, the mayor, the attorney general, the local newspaper – anything she could try to have my story heard. She went about it differently from how I would because she was a victim and deserved a voice. I was a potential liar and deserved scrutiny. Albeit a very believable one to have gotten as far with the police as I did. Pat had rights I was never given, and she could deal with it any way she pleased. She told everyone she knew in the missing-person arena. I understood her plight and determination.

If her sister was indeed the person in my father's make-shift grave, Pat had some of the facts askew. I hadn't shared everything with her to this point, but thought I'd go into more detail in my next email to her:

> *Good afternoon, Pat!*
>
> *I applaud your continued love and effort for Lynn. So so sweet. I'm still trying too. I've just begun to query Literary Agents to help sell my story to a publisher. I pray that through any money I could earn, I could hire the appropriate help to complete this all. I feel it's my duty.*
>
> *I never told you how the woman in the room was murdered. She was not beat to death [something Pat had assumed]. I withheld the facts of her death to shield you from any agony, but I fear that a beating to death is worse than the truth. My father always carried a knife in those days. He only swung at her once and the cut to her throat was enough to end her life.*
>
> *I hope that's not too difficult to hear, and I hope that it's better than a beating death. It's all terrible...all of it. If this is your sister, you should know the truth. Her life ended quickly.*
>
> *I want you to leave written, somewhere for me, the facts that you know support the woman I met is your sister. Should something happen to you, someone needs to know those facts.*

I sent her the PI reports I had from the investigation Mr. Peterson conducted a few years earlier, concerning her sister and the remaining family and friends.

In her first post to me, Pat said that she remembered talking with Detective Peterson. She continued, "I was not sure of my cousin Claire's report of seeing Madeline in 1972. I think she tried to please my mom who passed in 1991."

Mr. Peterson had concluded that the missing women buried in my father's field could have not been Lynn based on one individual's statement of seeing her in 1972. She added that her sister loved children, which, if this was the woman, made complete connection in that her kindness to me came through. Then, she agreed with the temperament I remembered when she said, "Her temperament stems from being born with water on the brain." Protectively stated, as a sister should. The more we emailed, the more things added up to assurances that we might just be on the right track.

We'd been emailing for over a year now. It was just after Christmas, and I asked Pat if she could please tell me why she knew this was her sister. She wouldn't tell me because she said that if the authorities knew she told me, they wouldn't believe I said it first. I had the emails with meta data that proved I first told Pat about – what she now confirmed for me.

On December 28, 2012, Pat decided, after a plea from me, to tell me why she believed it was her sister:

> Lyn had a signature with children she always played the purse game. Tucking her little legs in behind her. Lyn also would yell when she was upset with one of the brothers not doing his chores she would scream "I'll tell" "I'll tell," sound familiar? Madeline had little control of her emotions.

Tears ran down my face. Could it be her? How could it not be her with the "purse game." My heart released a lot, right there – even if we were wrong.

Pat continued:

Mom, Lyn and I went to see The Robe movie here in San Diego years ago. We lived here. She started to laugh and cry when Christ was being crucified and my Mom had to slap her to stop her. That is what the Dr's at Worcester Hospital told her to do.

Lyn's head was very large she wore bangs because of her large forehead. Lyn was a straight A student in school she had a photographic memory. Lynn trusted everyone and was overly friendly she had no common sense judgment not street wise in her personality. I was five years younger than her and was told by my Mom to keep an eye on her because some of the people she met were very wild and much different than her.

. . .

When you spoke of the purse game and the I'll tell I knew it was her. Madeline had a beautiful singing voice like my Mom. Now you know.

I still could not be certain the woman buried on my parents' place was Madeline without finding the bones, but her sister confirmed so much.

I emailed Pat the next day,

Oh, Pat...

I cannot stop crying after reading this email this morning. It is her. It absolutely has to be. I cannot create facts and have all these pieces match. I so want the ending of her life to have justification here. It is so wrong that the police won't listen to all these facts. Craig needs to be questioned.

I am so thankful to you and I had the opportunity to meet. It was divinely planned. Your words below release such deep tears in me. I was never comforted then, or now, or the terror that happened in that room. To know the lady that was with me there means more than I can ever tell you. She made me feel safe . . . as long as she could.

Thank you so much for sharing that. It is very healing to know more of the little lady that sat beside me those 40 years ago.
It is her.

Pat's warm reply:

It is only fair that you should know about those things you see. I knew it was Lyn the minute you said it about the purse game and the I'll tell was so significant it was Lyn I knew it was. I was hoping that one of those police officers would get the message, but they tend to buff it off like they do not want to hear the truth. Jodie, I am glad my sister was with you and you with her. I am very glad we became friends.

We will prevail in all this Jodie it just takes time and patience. I knew it was her no doubt in my mind. Too many things that you said fit the puzzle.

This was what my mother said when I went to her with my memories, and later, proof. When we first met Mr. Peterson, I had my mother with us. He asked her, "Why do you believe your daughter." My mother said, "She has too many factually correct pieces to not listen to. She knew the cars, where her father hid important items in the house, and so on."

Even though I hadn't yet turned four, my mind kept me safe. It housed the scary parts and only returned them to me when I could heal.

Pat finished her email with, "Dry your tears and know that you gave her comfort in her last hours. Hugs, Pat."

If my search had been in anger and wanting my father and Craig to pay, I wouldn't have fought so hard to find her.

Pat and I emailed each other for several years and built a friendship. I believe she's gone now. I'm so thankful we found rest with each other.

Scratching memories revealed more to me than I wanted in the following months.

Twenty

Searching for Myself

"I came to explore the wreck. The words are purposes. The words are maps. I came to see the damage that was done and the treasures that prevail."
—*Diving in the Wreck* by Adrienne Rich

In my late forties, my third marriage had failed. Healing had taken me far enough to convince me not to stay in deceitful relationships, but it hadn't taken me far enough not to choose them in the first place. It was time to dig a little deeper.

The road leading to my parents' house is easy to miss. An old country one, imbedded in deep-wooded acres, which at one time was graveled only with rocks big enough to gouge the bottom of our bare feet during summertime. It was a trek city folks found too far to visit often, which was probably why my father picked it. The driveway had been an old logging route years earlier and Daddy had taken an entire summer to retrace the outline and make it the new path to his kingdom: the kingdom of the blind. Armed with a Ford pickup, a chainsaw, miscellaneous tools, and his four kids (captive to him as laborers), we carved our way through those doomed, deciduous trees and rebuilt that road.

I came to the bend in the road and took the hidden gateway to the house I was raised in. Dad had passed away a few years earlier, and it was now a little easier for a short time to make the trip to Mom, but his presence had undeniably seeped into the territory. Just the descent down that long driveway triggered shivers in me, with its snaking ways weaving through his land. The road, a sneak preview of death, whose wrenching turns and darkened corners initiated a state of agitation before one came upon his mansion.

I walked into the house and it smelled like the food of my childhood -- the aroma of oven-fried chicken. That familiar conundrum of superficial comfort and lurking pain pricked my senses. I've always loved my mom's cooking, there was warmth in her food – not, however, in her eyes. The pain of living in her marriage for over fifty years -- as an accomplice and a victim -- had taken a toll on her. Through the years she probably tried to muster what she could to give us children the belief that things were finally okay, but the decay in her soul crept through in ghastly anger that would abruptly appear – the thousand accumulated storms of her immured life.

Growing up, we caught glimpses of her most often when she was home on the weekends. We could often find her leaning over a coffee-soiled linen tablecloth, tackling a mixing bowl of foodstuff, lost in impenetrable silence. When we went out together as a family, which was infrequent, appearances became paramount. My mother upheld our façade by mandating proper clothing for family outings and sanctioned smiles to hide the stench of betrayal. My thin brown hair, which was usually untended to and in gnarls, was combed only on the occasion when other people might be around.

My nephew and his kids were visiting on this day too. I wanted desperately to try and learn to enjoy being around my family home, but my stomach tightly bound itself into knots. I tried to comfort myself by the presence of others in the house and kept reminding myself that I wasn't alone, reassuring my frightened inner child that Dad was gone now. But the thoughts did little to soothe me. It was as if every label I'd been given, all the fears and every lost dream, was trying to latch itself onto me like some dynastic specter.

I was relieved from my inner-most thoughts and fears when my mother called us in for supper. Knowing I had been roaming her halls, she staged the conversation to keep me in line and not keep time for my questions. Manipulation thinly veiled behind boring small talk.

After dinner, I roamed the house that I had not been welcome in for years. My father often mouthed the words, "You are always welcome here, Jodie," but they meant that my reality needed to stay on the other side of their front door, so I seldom went. With him gone, I longed to search through his things. I wanted to find something that would give me clues, maybe a fact or evidence of the past. I'd been there on and off through the years, but most of the visits were confrontational. I'd storm in, demanding Daddy's truth, him never giving it to me. Sometimes, these stopovers wen````t better than others.

Once, at eighteen, after an abusive episode with my first husband, I drove up to see my parents, still seeking a form of protection from them. I stopped and bought a box of donuts, drove up at 5 am, and stood under their window calling up to them to awaken -- something like a lost lover would do.

Living without your family is a tormenting choice. It was my decision, but it left me miserably lonely at times.

I stopped by another time needing familial connection and this time my dad offered me a drink and asked if I wanted to sing old country tunes on his cheap karaoke machine with him. I was thrilled! I hadn't been the apple of his eye for so long. To make him happy was always a longing in my heart --that hadn't diminished. The song he picked first was "Delta Dawn." The lyrics passed through my lips, "She's forty-one and her Daddy still calls her baby." I was the only one my father called baby. I loved the words and hated them simultaneously. I longed to run into his arms and bash him in the head at the same time. As a good friend of mine used to say, I didn't know whether to shit or wind my watch. I just knew I loved him.

Eventually, my father no longer referred to me as his baby. I don't know if I took the right away from him or he took that right away from me, but I became just Jodie. It hurt. A lot. I had endured severely for that title. It was earned and I deserved it.

One day after church service a particular urge to go to my father gripped me. By this time in my life, I had begun to listen to the very small drum beat inside. It was the same consonance I had begun to hear, though indistinctly, at eight years old. A drum beat unlike any other and I knew it was the undeniable rhythm of love from a God who was very different from the god of my father.

I went to church often, as it did offer some relief from the constant storms and as I learned to trust this new God, I tried to listen to the voice I was hearing that called me to go visit my father on this day. I was alone as I usually was in those days and terrified of the man, so I tried to ignore the urging but it persisted and deep inside I knew I needed to take some of my strength back from him.

Good counselors will tell you that confrontation is a powerful tool in recovery. Knowing this, I took the long drive up the mountain that day. The twisting roads seemed to mimic my spiraling thoughts. However, my body betrayed my efforts. My breathing became forced, my heart pounded, and my hands shook awkwardly. I wasn't going to make it physically without stopping to calm my nerves. I hated the fact that I would show up a mess. He might believe that I wasn't as confident as I acted.

I found some random sports bar I'd never been to and pulled in. I ordered a drink. What the hell was I going for? I needed some kind of plan, so I started making a list. Three drinks later I had written out a list of topics to tackle with him. February 27, 2005, a Sunday, I wrote:

- What hotel did you & Craig go to?
- Why let him do stuff? How did that help you . . . or – was it just about hurting me?
- Before you die – I want you to know how much pain & damage you've caused – me – my girls – your other children

– their children – great grands – ALL YOU............ Ripple
effect to us

My faith, intertwined with liquid courage and my bar-drawn list of
questions, was going to get me through.

I walked into my father's home with a determination to confront
him about his friendship with Craig but kept a pleasant demeanor so
I wouldn't be dismissed. I followed him quietly into the room that he
parked himself in. I asked him for a drink (he always had something,
even if clandestinely). It would initiate common ground between us.
We both sat. Me on the sectional couch and Dad in his chair. It forced
us to face each other. He asked me what I wanted and said my mom
had some booze as well. I didn't know my mom drank in these years.
He scoffed a bit and said, "Oh, she drinks." She did?" My mother has
a remarkable way of hiding her own evil and showcasing my father's.
She refers to herself as the "white sheep" of her family. I also had a
strong desire to keep her vicious ways hidden as well in those days –
they were way too painful to see. I truly didn't know much about my
mother other than our earliest years together and to my father's point,
I really didn't know her at all.

I'd left my handwritten notes in the car so I tried to pull up the list I'd
written in my mind's eye, attempting to appear as calm and natural as I
could. I pretended I wanted to be his friend. He wasn't the only master
of disguise. He sat on a weathered chair in the old garage that had been
converted into a room. On the wall above of him was a picture of him
and Craig standing by an old car Dad called the *Iron Maiden* – some
kind of homage to his fixation with Germany and Hitler. I stood, took
it off the wall, and told him I remembered Craig well. I asked him to
chat about his memory of the car and Craig's friendship. It didn't take
us anywhere valuable so I asked him if I could keep the picture and I
moved on. This is a copy of the picture in Craig's story album.

My next question was one he wouldn't like and that I hadn't written
down. My dad lived in a manufactured world when it came to his own
family of origin, always telling us what a great family he came from.

Maybe he did come from a loving home, and he just couldn't accept it. Many people can't. Or maybe the religion he used to hide behind all of his life he'd learned from his parents and the great bible belt.

"Who were your parents to you?" I told him I needed to know because if they had mistreated him, it might help me understand why he hated us – his family. I could no longer contain my tears and they streamed down my face. I looked into his eyes, searching for answers. Would he try to explain to me that religion was a tool that he was taught to hide his own past and so naturally he handed it to us?

He stood and came toward me. With his fists clenched and his jaw rock solid, he said, "Get the fuck out of my house." My father never used the word fuck (it's probably why I like using it).

I wasn't going to let him hit me that day, so I gave him a good shove. He fell backward onto the couch. When he landed his body slumped to one side. I told him with a shaky, but steady voice, "Dad, don't make me hurt you."

He was now a pathetic old man. A mere shadow of the man I once knew. He'd lost a leg to diabetic complications and that seemed to be a great indication of what was going on inside the man -- decay and rot. The punishment for his previous actions now seeped through his pores and was literally eating him alive. Obviously, these visits didn't leave much time to look through nostalgic items.

This day visiting his house offered me a luxury I hadn't had with him alive: freedom to snoop. Healing isn't about pointing fingers. Sorting through childhood family dynamics, as well as family heirlooms and belongings, had to help locate my inner-most self. I really wanted my father's computer, but my mother wouldn't concede. It surely would have been a fascinating albeit ominous journey. I was looking for a way to validate my existence in this family but the deeper issue I had was validating my story -- who I had been in that house and what I had witnessed --not the fraudulent bullshit they represented. Wasn't it my birthright to share my own story? I didn't need to be a part of them -- I was actually very grateful to have earned some freedom to be far away from them. I felt like a stranger lurking into corners I wasn't invited into, but that didn't stop me from trying, and it made my mother nervous.

Around the house, it was as if evil had been pulverized into a fine dust and collected on all the cluttered stacks that lay around. An old table with a phone, an answering machine, and a pad of paper. Who might call there?

They lived such different lives. The first life full of loud music, beautiful clothes, good looking people partying and the next was like the Mormon Tabernacle choir had abducted them into some weird religious cult. So, I couldn't even begin to dream up what kind of messages might be saved there. Table lamps burned on every surface. An eerily illumination cast a sallow glow onto the room, making everything look sickly and dreamlike. My father had covered half of the wall in untreated wood and had built a shelf on top that separated the wood from the sheetrock so Mom could display family mementos. The pictures had been prominently displayed, showcasing a family destroyed. An ominous presence permeated the rough wood that clung to those walls. There wasn't much in this room at this point as it was used as a sort of parlor now. In their first life, this was where they kept the pool table. Lit-up beer signs with moving pieces clung to the walls. Next to it, a pool cue rack and a stereo blaring Glen Campbell and Johnny Cash. I liked that room best. At least it was authentic.

Next, I went into what used to be my brother's bedroom. I quickly remembered the distinct smell of that room when it was his, the waterbed he had, and all the moments he had asked me if I remembered sharing with him there. I became nauseated. It had been converted to a storage room. Packed full of boxes and other debris. A few filing cabinets stacked along one of the walls piqued my interest. My parents weren't dumb, so I didn't imagine there'd be a smoking gun in the papers I wanted to rifle through, but maybe there'd be something of value.

I opened one drawer and thumbed through the files and then browsed another. They were nicely organized with labels. I stopped looking when I realized the futility of searching in such a commonplace location.

In the new dining room addition, I found my mother sitting on the far end of a hulking table that follow the entire length of this new dining area. The giant, overstated table seemed to symbolize her egotistical notion of family. She had been going through things herself, plastic containers lying sporadically around the dining room. The items thrown about in these containers looked much more personal and I asked if I could have a look. She nodded and I began going through a trove of unknown objects. I was eager to see what memories were housed there but wasn't prepared for all the captured times that I'd never been a part of. I'd chosen to be away from my family for some twenty years by now, but it still profoundly saddened me.

I picked up one photo and then another. Some of these people I had never even seen before. Other pictures were past reminders of who I had once been. There were cards o' plenty floating amongst the pictures. I picked up one, it was from a great grandkid saying: "Happy Valentine's Day." I flipped another paper over, and it was a poem written by my sister, expressing a child's love to a sick mother.

Then, I opened a card that was written by me to my father some thirty years earlier. It read:

> *"Dad – I feel I should write and warm your heart, and yet tell you that I am not the one who can heal you. I cannot be your comforter or confidant. I can only be a daughter who loves you. A daughter who cares deep enough to say, I know I need to be away."*

My mind raced to remember the words I had penned so many years before. I couldn't believe I'd found the courage to write them. I could see my unwieldy attempt to forge distance between myself and his control. This period had to be after my father told me that he didn't want me to stay with Richard, my first husband and the father of my children. Dad did not like my ownership betrothed to another man.

Around this time, Richard had thrown a glass at me one night when we were at my grandmother's house drinking (whiskey, and I still don't like whiskey!). My older sister had asked me if I had dated a boy in her class (this predated Richard). He was a good-looking football player and most girls wanted to date him. I met him some time after he'd graduated, and she was just curious. I answered that I had dated him and added that his silhouette in the night light showed off his great body. I learned very quickly that I still had no freedom to speak – just because I was out of my father's house hadn't given me freedom because I unknowingly had given it to another man.

No sooner had I got the words out of my mouth than I felt something smash and shatter on my cheek. It was thick carnival glass that had made its way to the present from the 1920s. I ran to my grandmother's bedroom and looked in the mirror. I was horrified to see the entire left side of my face starting under my eye draped in blood and my eye was already swelling shut. The blunt force on my face left gaping wounds that would require future plastic surgery and left lifetime scars on my face.

So, in my father's mind, he was doing his part to protect me and regain his control. You see, my dad wasn't just a murderer, he was a man who believed he protected the ones he loved at any cost. He sat me down at his kitchen table that day thirty years from the penned message in this card and frankly told me that he'd spent hours walking his property. He explained how he'd found a place to put Richard's body where it would never be found. My parents owned about forty acres of land, so it was no stretch of imagination to believe he'd located another burial plot.

My card continued:

During these rough waters know that I love you but know that my absence is truly the best. I release you into the hands of your loving and deeply caring wife. Draw from her kindness.

What? Who was I? It sounded as if I were writing to my ex-lover, not my father. I was releasing him to his wife. Wasn't she also my mother? Deeply loving and caring?

Tenderize your heart with her moving words. It will be in her arms,
Dad, that you will find what you need.

Oh, for God's sake! I wanted to reach back and slap myself. Where were those who were supposed to help me? I wasn't the parent. I was their child. How much I had grown since I wrote those words. A care-taker to my father wasn't a strong enough definition for what I had scratched on to that card.

My mind quickly retraced all the years I had mimicked this role with the men in my life. I didn't know what I needed when I sent that card to Dad, but I did know one thing -- I needed to be free from him. I didn't read anger in my sentences, only a desire to be released from his choking hold on my life.

Then, the false religion I'd been taught that shrouded my father and mother with secrecy leaked through my pen:

As you walk through these waters know that Christ is with you.
I will continue to pray and do all that is best. Allow the Father to guide
your steps. He knows and has your best interests in His heart.
United we will indeed stand. The past forgiven, we march on. Love-- Me."

Holy crap! My path had taken me so far from those hollow empty words. Dad thrived on believing that if he quoted enough scripture behind the wall of religious ways, he might make it through the decep-tive ocean that surrounded him. With his past forgiven, he taught each of us that we could not discuss it.

Year after year, I would seek a different kind of God. A God who was real enough to somehow show me He cared. A God who didn't shy away from the cold, ugly facts of my life but one who wanted to bring them to the surface, purge them in a way that would free me. A God who could prove He genuinely loved me. Not the god of my father who bled dry the grounds watered with truth.

I got in my car and drove away from that abandoned castle of lies. The time there could not help but whirl the disquiet within me and how it all began.

Twenty-One

She Loves Me, She Loves Me Not

**"Throw away the lights, the definitions
And say of what you see in the dark"**
—*The Man with the Blue Guitar* **by Wallace Stevens**

"Your mother hated you." My counselor's face was pained as he said the words. He paused and fell silent, the requisite irritating lull, and braced for my reaction to his painfully overt summation of the writing assignment he'd given me at our last appointment.

Not knowing what to say, I was both stunned and relieved. Was it a truth I could handle or was it one I would run from – as I'd been doing my whole life? I walked out and didn't return to his office for a year. I couldn't face the deepest truth of his words. I had shared my secrets with him but to hear them decrypted and recited back to me felt like a betrayal.

A relationship with a counselor was the very last fucking thing I wanted. I had come through a mire of a shit storm in my life but held onto the belief that I could get through this alone. That I could pass for *normal* if I tried hard enough. Going to a counselor proved weakness, vulnerability, and cowardice and I wanted nothing to do with it. Those cowards who sat in their pious chairs and called themselves helpers were just a bunch of rotten skeptics waiting to judge. Their appetite for rumors and stories guided their journeys to hang those shingles on their doors and open for business. Therapy was a spectator sport filled with voyeuristic onlookers seeking a vicarious hit from a world they are too protected to experience. Of all the fakes in the world, the ones hiding behind their own percipience might be the worst. I wanted nothing to do with these strangers.

But year after year, I found a need for a physician. Not the kind of physician that you see to heal a broken bone or help a back injury. I needed someone who knew the scope of the human psyche. They had to understand behavior -- why certain causes and effects worked the way they did. I needed answers far beyond what I could find anywhere else. No one seemed to know the solution to the riddle my soul hid – its nest of memories, a tangle of experience. So, I'd have to deny my desire to ridicule these gossip junkies and find one I could trust. Oh, I'd ridicule them anyway, but I had to start somewhere, and as you've read, Foster was just the place.

This therapist was unlike any I had spent time with. He appeared like Mr. Rogers -- all sweaters and well-worn loafers -- but I put aside my judgments of him and set out to do the work. He was a different kind of therapist. I liked him. I couldn't help but like him because he was helping me. For real. His treatment was different, and it felt like he genuinely cared. I had no idea what he thought and frankly didn't give a damn. That was what made this relationship so good. I didn't have to care, and it seemed to me that he did.

After I worked with Foster for years, he'd finally given me this mother assignment. He'd try through the years to get me to chat about her, but I wouldn't. I mustered enough strength to make an appointment to go back.

Initially, I confused his softness for meekness. But soon, I began to appreciate his tenderness and tenacity to tell me the truth – the two qualities that lead me to trust him but also trust myself. Our first few meetings he spent setting up basic rules, explaining we were going to get intimate in his office. Ha! I would never sleep with him. The truth was -- a nice man like Foster would never choose a scrapper like me. He had explained that therapists like him believed deeply in building relationships with their patients – often called a therapeutic alliance. By building and experiencing a secure attachment with Foster, apparently, I could begin to feel safe enough to start to resolve some of my old traumas and maybe evolve my old model of relating. Odd -- I was paying for a friend. I didn't understand yet that the intimacy he referred to was not sex but a new way of relating built on mutual trust and respect.

He made it clear from the beginning that I had to be respectful of my appointments. If I missed one, I had to pay. Ugh – I didn't like the accountability to him, but ultimately learned why it was necessary.

His office was in an old Craftsman-style house, which had been partitioned into multiple offices. The waiting room was littered with the usual counselor's office stuff: magazines, self-help books on healing, a book on dream interpretation, and the ever-familiar water cooler tower to quench the parched mouth of the nervous patient. I'd been to many of these offices over the years. I picked up a book on dreams and paged through it impatiently. Being here felt like purgatory – all this waiting. The walls needed to be painted, the chairs replaced, and the broken-down couch donated.

Resentment grew in me. I hated that I needed to be there. I would return to this place year after year, time after time – sometimes hopeful, often incensed. But, somewhere beyond this dingy room was my salvation. I would live a life that held beauty. I'd have time to smell the distinct fragrance of a rose and be free from these counseling walls. No one else could help me decipher the code hidden in the deepest marrow of my bones. But maybe Foster could.

Flipping the switch wired to Mr. Foster's office, indicating my arrival, I felt a combination of anger and fear. Thankfully, my brooding thoughts were interrupted by the sudden yet gentle opening of the hallway door. Out came the familiar face I was beginning to love and with a confirming gesture, I was ushered in. A strong precautionary shift of my soul had occurred to trust a man who had only a sincere intention of helping me find one more piece of the puzzle to my past.

His office always remained the same. If something about it changed, we had that discussion before we could begin. If something was out of order, my heart steadied on the change. I had to be careful to determine if it was still safe here. Sometimes, any change meant dread. Not in that room necessarily but generally speaking. I had to be sure before we proceeded.

"Were you scared when you told me my mother hated me? Or did you know I was ready to hear you?" I had been waiting for months to ask him this.

His answer was as prescribed as his requisite collection of books staggered on the shelves next to him. "You can never be sure, but I was hoping you would be ready to go there."

Foster had been trying to get me to talk about my mother for years. We discussed the debauchery of my father time and again. The woman who had gone missing in 1968 who was now buried on my parents' property. The pedophiles who dominated our home. The shared victimization of the children with my dad and his best friend. But my mother? I just didn't want to go there. She was all I had left that felt normal.

Until the day he looked at me squarely and said, "But she wasn't normal, was she Jodie?"

I searched his office trying to avoid the penetrating contact with the truth. Since I had driven myself to his office, walked up the stairs, down the side path, back up yet another set of stairs that led to the first door into the dimly lit waiting area, pushed the lever on the wall to indicate I was there – surely, I was prepared for what waited for me when the man with the kind eyes opened his office door welcoming me in. But it was never easy. Easy would be to die daily in tiny increments by denying the truth. No, this was not easy. Not even close to it.

"She did hate me, Foster. I just don't know why."

Our fifty minutes were coming to a well-awaited close and it was time for me to find a quick escape. He encouraged me, as he always did, to drink less and continue to let my story be free in my body, which included being free to infiltrate my mind. This was a terrifying prospect, as nightmares had plagued me for years. I came to see him to avoid scary dreams, not induce them. I thanked him politely for saying the worst words I'd ever had someone say to me and walked out of his office. On the way out, the waiting room morphed into a place of comfort – comfort that I was nearly out of that office and back to my getaway car.

I opened the door with the slumped sinking weight of my body. Slowly, the bright light of day peeked through. I paused and pushed the door ever so slightly to delay the reality that waited for me. I walked out onto the wooden deck that led to a small courtyard area. The fog of PTSD was now encompassing the grassy courtyard and casting its distinctive shadow on everything. I paused, watching the delicate sky dying. The haze felt frightening and unsafe, but I had become familiar with its glow. It made me feel outside of my body, out of control in so many ways. I kept walking, trying to digest what the fuck the coming days would look like. Should I let the dead carcass of memory lie dormant as I strongly desired it to? Or did I go exploring on the advice of his proverbial wisdom? To stay put wasn't a reasonable answer. I had been in an eighteen-year abusive marriage and had since staggered through miserable relationship after miserable relationship. I had to go forward and try.

The problem with memory is you never know what precariously obnoxious time it will present itself. It seldom happens while you're sitting by the warmth of a fire, candle throwing its beautiful scent into the air, jazz music softly playing while you wait for it to arrive so you can package the bastard up and throw it away. Nope – that's not how it happens and that is not how these memories returned either.

Months earlier Foster's words haunted me as I tried to stay busy. This easiest way to turn off reality was to throw myself into work. Work is like hitting a golf ball –takes your mind off anything else. I only have a high school diploma but have a great mind that had been overly exercised as a child and was now quite strong. I started as a receptionist in a law firm and moved my way twenty-five years later into management. But his ghostly words haunted me as I advanced in my career and buried myself in work. Our sessions followed me as I tried to stay present in my relationships – at work and otherwise. His words woke me in the morning and were the last thing I heard when I fell asleep. I wanted to find a way to dismiss this path that had opened before. I wanted to believe there was a way through this memory without exploring it. I had explored so many by now, wasn't that enough? So, I didn't spend much time looking for it but as the past always does, it came looking for me.

By the time I reached eighteen, married my first husband, and got away from my parents, no part of myself remained. I had lost 60 pounds by now and was very attractive. My shining dark hair had the feathery wave of the Farah Fawcett do in the 80s. But I was simply a shell of a person, dressed up in a drab blue monochromatic religious uniform issued by my folks, with my head resting face first in a bowl of porridge -- lifeless. Even at thirty-five, after having two beautiful children and leaving their father, my husband, in pursuit of my truth, I still couldn't remember who I was. Yes, I was a wife and a mother, but who was Jodie? This wasn't a classic narcissistic form of self-absorption. I had gained a sense of emotional autonomy by now and it wasn't about judgment or condemnation. I simply needed to find the real me. What was this glimmer of a torturous past my soul was trying to find? I had to know. It wouldn't leave me alone. The hunt for the truth was my destination and beyond that destination was my selfhood.

I began to learn the hard way that the influence of deception was on their side. On top of the abuse and trauma, denial heaps on more hurt by requiring a person to alienate herself from reality and her own experience. In troubled families, abuse and neglect are permitted.

It's the talking about them that is forbidden.

Twenty-Two

Smoke n' Perfume

"And who will remember the rememberers?"
—Yehuda Amichai

My legs weren't working, and I couldn't talk. This returning memory was ugly and raw. My work with Foster was working.

I was in my father's arms as he carried me through my grandmother's front door, the porch making its distinct creaking noises. Built in 1918, the house was a good design for someone who didn't much like housework. Knowing each groan of that house intimately gave my grandmother some sense of control and protection. My dad trudged inside and without a word, placed me on her weathered couch. My grandmother reached toward me, her warm eyes and slight smile announcing her love. I couldn't respond. Her light blue eyes dimmed and flashed with worry, but the familiar smell of aging cigarette smoke and heavy perfume gave me instant comfort.

Grandma Eleanor was my mother's mom. She had come to this country from Finland with her parents and three older sisters. Soon after, her parents returned to Finland, leaving all sisters in America to fend for themselves. It was not uncommon in those days, but still a very brutal way to grow up -- fending to find a way in an unknown land.

This built strength in her, albeit not the kind she would have asked for. The strength I saw in my grandmother had come from a grueling denial of her own pain and a life that never validated it, but she had a way of showing me love -- unlike my mother -- and it was her simple kindness that carried me through those years.

She too had sisu.

In the safety of her house, my small despondent body could now find rest. As I lay limply on the end of her couch, my grandmother spoke my name once more. I couldn't respond but could hear her. Her voice offered me hope that she may just be my rescue angel – at long last. When her extended hand was not met with mine, her face distorted. She was furious. She knew very well who my father could be. All her one hundred pounds lunged at him. She threw her finger in his face and screamed – hurling accusation and demanding answers about what they had done to me. His face became stonelike and the slight twitch in his cheek was evidence that he'd listened enough. In his usual style, he scoffed at her and strode out the door. Relief filled my body when he finally left.

It may have been a few hours or a few days before I landed, in this state, on her couch. Memory doesn't date stamp and pain blurs the details, but it must have been early Sunday morning in that tiny, dismal home of ours when my father decided it was time to drive me to her because I had become an inconsolable nuisance to them.

I can almost be sure that it was Sunday because in those days, my father seldom worked, and my mother never missed a day on the job. Occasionally, Mother piled her thick blonde hair high on top of her head and would run a bath. She would make me stand and watch her bathe. She wanted me to know that she had a pretty good figure, and she shared that detail with me often. Work was important to her because she was never going to be poor again. The story of her having only two dresses to alternate for school etched an impenetrable desire in her for more.

The three of them were together so it was certainly their hedonistic play date and my mother loved to be included.

My father called me into their bedroom. His voice was deep and connected to whatever desire he was feeling. It never entered my mind to not follow his voice that sounded deftly like Satan beckoning me. It was different this day because he seldom abused me in his bedroom. There was no need to – he had full reign of the house. Anything different made me suspicious (it still does!). As my little legs turned the corner of the open door, I wanted to turn and run. All three of them were in bed naked. They were acting like they were drunk or something. The room was chaotic, and they were all in a great mood. Mornings were usually a time of hungover darkness in our home, so it was unusual for them to be up and happy when I was called in. My mother was standing on the bed laughing. As I walked in, she strolled past me and went down the hall.

Dad called me up to the bed where he and his best friend Craig were lying. He put me in the middle of them and caressed my hair as he often did. Stroking my face, he told me he loved me and that it was going to be okay. In that moment, everything was okay. I always believed him. In fact, I knew I was loved more than any other little girl – right then, at that moment. It was like a calm before the storm, and I was happy to be beside him. Then, my mother entered the room, almost dancing. She was having a great time with these boys. But now, I was part of the cast. She never liked that my father gave me attention. Her jealousy was always present, and it never weakened toward me. I knew only one thing -- this wasn't going to end well.

This wasn't the first time they had done this. The first threesome gang bang was different. My father was the receiver of pleasure. Craig was just an onlooker. The twist – Mom. These boys had their sexual fill of me and my siblings while she worked. Secretly, I believed she'd help if she knew.

Turning the corner to their room that morning killed whatever hope remained of help.

Her position above me gave her an advantage to pin me down. She cleverly used one knee to push my head into full submission so I couldn't squirm. As my father began to rape me, my mind went berserk, and my body flailed out of control. That just forced my father to apply more force on my tiny ankles.

When he stopped raping me, I was supposed to get out, but my left foot wouldn't work to take me to the door. Mom made a joke of the whole thing, telling me it was just a game and reminded me that I was not hurt.

When they were finished with me this time, it was more than a strained ankle. I couldn't move. Craig brought me to my room that day. The invasive attack was more than I could bear. I don't know how long I stayed that way, catatonic. The memory I chose to carry forward was the way it ended.

My mom's brother, Uncle Dick, was monumental in his strength of love that he offered me. When I was left catatonic as a child and brought to my grandmother, it was his great love that scooped me up, took me to his apartment in Portland, and cared for me. I'll never remember his words, but I have never forgotten his love. I believed as a little girl, I'd get to live with him forever. But that was dashed when my father showed up that sunny day on my uncle's rooftop courtyard and told me I'd have to leave with him. When that memory returned, I found myself plastered on the floor, unable to gather myself, very close to catatonic again.

I am forever grateful for this beautiful love my uncle and I shared.

I don't need to sugarcoat my reality because my faith is strong. Free to declare the truth of my life, acknowledging affliction does not diminish my faith in God. Rather, it proves it.

In a dream many years ago, I was intently watching a big white spider lay very delicate eggs. After the eggs were laid, she backed into her dark corner to watch over them. These egg sacks were nestled together in a strong web. As I watched the sacks, they were each thriving with hundreds of eggs that were incubating evil.

I knew I needed to kill those eggs, but the white mother spider sat looking from her perched distance. I wasn't sure how to accomplish it. I decided to act because the birth of those eggs would bring much wickedness. I thought if I could just reach in and quickly pinch them strong enough, they would die. I had to try.

As the dream continued, it became clear to me that the spider was my mother, and the eggs were hers. That gave me an added burden in wanting to protect those I loved and not let evil continue. I had to find a way to demolish the evil that would be birthed. Now, it was unborn and the evil -- underdeveloped.

In the end, I decided I had to do something so those eggs could not hatch. I reached toward the eggs with a determination to quickly extinguish the evil they held by pinching them. With one swift move, the white spider bit the back of my hand with a mighty force. It was so powerful it jolted me awake.

I was trembling, the back of my hand felt the piercing, but at least I was now awake.

I recognize God's power and control over my life. I also recognize that I didn't fight my mother's flesh and bones but the evil control she allows. She grew evil with pleasure. Maybe the illusion of power brings her to believe she has ultimate control and can relieve herself of her own pain. I'm not sure why and I don't care anymore. I left her at the feet of God.

Evil will not be following my future generations.

Twenty-Three

My Mother's Dowry

"By the pricking of my thumbs, something wicked this way comes."
— William Shakespeare, Macbeth

I continued to let the truth seek me out and vowed to meet it – even if the road was long and dark and lonely and filled with tripwire and pitfalls. Memories don't return to the mind with one telling like an old man sitting you down and recalling in full chronological detail all the things that had happened in his life. Just as I've interrupted my telling of this memory, that was how interrupted they have been to my life, to my peace and to my health.

The memories of being gang raped by my parents and their close friend would stay buried for nearly fifty years. As Foster had done time and time before, he led me down the path of my next phase of healing. I am forever grateful to him. He only asked me questions and listened. He didn't hypnotize me, nor did he use any form of quackery or cajolery. Skeptical of any kind of therapy that might produce or procure a created memory, I'd worked long and slow to ensure a process that I could trust and one I knew would be true. Foster is a skilled listener -- trained to hear which path we should explore next -- and he felt this was a good path. It was a byway that I had tried to keep hidden.

After that writing exercise about my mother, months passed before my mind and heart felt safe enough to open. Why wasn't it enough to just find the hidden grief of that day? But I knew what was coming next, and it was too late to stop now and turn back to a time when I didn't know. It's like that country song, "I wish I didn't know now what I didn't know then." I would even question Foster, surmising that if he told me I could stop – I would. He would simply say, "You know it's too late now to go back." During these periods, I usually drank more than I should and truly did just about anything to escape. And not just drinking. It was married men and mayhem. It was going to church and trying to do better and then doing it all over again to escape the agony of the memories that loomed over my life, carrying my ghosts through every decision that affected my health, my happiness, and future These were fucking hard times and I didn't judge myself for how I got through them. I don't believe God was judging me either.

The body keeps the score, as they now say. Hell yes, it sure does. Sometime after this work with Foster, I had a numbing throb of nerves in my upper arms like a band was wrapped around them, tightened severely, and restricting blood flow. It felt as if that band had been in place way too long. It woke me up with its annoying persistence. I hadn't injured them so couldn't figure out what was going on with my body. After several weeks of this anguish, my husband insisted I go to a physical therapist. But the PT couldn't determine what the problem was either. In fact, he mentioned that overusing muscles wouldn't cause them to hurt in this way. I also went to see an acupuncturist. I liked the feeling when I left, but my arms continued to ache with phantom pain.

I'd made the decision long before to continue at all costs when memories came. I'd learned to be grateful for them most of the time. Owning them gave me a sense of belonging -- belonging to myself. I'd also learned how to control the speed at which they returned. I could choose to drag the process out, trying to keep them buried for another year, maybe longer. I'd stalled so many times, hoping with everything in me that I was wrong, but didn't fight that old battle --anymore. I'd battle that demon and won years ago. Avoiding the pain of the facts never got easier. I hoped to slightly change the facts, making them a little easier, have some hugs built into to the flimsy fabric of my childhood – some random act of kindness. But the truth has a savage way of asserting itself. No matter how you slice and dice it, it'll surface again and again, with a steady path that unfortunately stays the same. You can't really avoid them.

After my last divorce, I hadn't dated at all. I told Foster I'd most likely be alone for another ten years. He said, "I don't think you will, Jodie. You're a different person now."

He was right. I had grown.

I met a man who couldn't have been more different than me. My grandmother always said, "still waters run deep" and that was this guy. His name is Jeff. We married. No longer was I alone on this journey at long last.

I crawled into bed, kissed Jeff goodnight, and settled into my lengthy sleep-inducing ritual. I did fall asleep and with it came a strong wind that blew the fog out of my mind. My fear of returning to that scene lifted in the early morning hours of that night. Then, I was jolted awake to the answer to my riddled arms. I saw it: my mother was straddling me, and the weight of her knees left my arms broken. There it was, the prescription for my pain, at 3 am: welcome back to your childhood. Are you kidding me? This is what's wrong with my arms?

My brain, seemingly set on fire, tugged at a loose thread of an old memory and I was right back in the moment that caused me so much grief to begin with. All it takes is a familiar smell, a taste of your past, a sound that ripples through you like a gunshot.

I got up and the reality of moving through yet another horrific memory pursued me as I sipped my coffee. The recalled memories left my eyes broken; they couldn't even force a blink. More accurately stated, my heart was broken, again. I couldn't stop remembering.

For weeks, I moved through that memory and endured endless waves of emotion. I struggled with deep anxiety that was being driven by a constriction on my arms and chest. I found it continually hard to catch my breath and my arms continued to ache, but I felt a sense of pride at how my body had held all of it for me until a time it could bring me back to this memory. Only the innermost part of my being and God knew when that time would be. It was time to take the garbage out.

After my father had finished with me, my mother, in anger, took her turn. She'd held me down before and allowed my father to rape me, but she'd never been the recipient of the pleasure – just a bystander. My heart pounded as I watched her climb up on me and straddle my tiny body. It felt like an elephant mounting a mouse. Not that I would have fought her, I had no strength, but she insisted on restraining me anyway. I want to hate her for what happened next – but I don't.

She forced her vagina into my face. I had no idea what she was doing or why. Not only was I pinned under this whale, but I also couldn't find my breath. The air was being zapped out of me and I was losing consciousness. I don't think it took very long for my mind to fail me and give up. I passed out. I am thankful for that. It saved me from a longer torture.

When the surreal episode ended and I came to, I could hear and see but my body wouldn't move. A gripping feeling ensued that I was broken. Physically broken. I didn't know what to do. I was literally catatonic and, in a haze, not knowing if I was dead or alive. If I were alive, I would be able to move. This must be another state of evil and I was stuck there in a grotesque fog – completely comatose. I could hear my mother telling me to go to my room but couldn't move. I wanted out of there in the worst way, but my body wouldn't respond.

I hated my mother as I heard her mocking my inability to move. Finally, Craig picked me up and took me to another room. I was so relieved to leave that dungeon. I didn't remember my dad being in the room with us while I stared at the ceiling, which was strange too because he was always the ring master. I just wanted to go away from my mom in the worse way possible. I use the word hate, but I really don't think I understood hate then. I was too small. I just knew she didn't like me, and I didn't much like her.

I was my mother's dowry to her husband. A gift from her womb to a man she treasured. Mommy wounds aren't talked about as much as father wounds are, but they are strong and just as deep. The betrayal from a person who carried you in her body can only be surmised by a child as life threatening. She brought me into this world, and she could take me out. I was left with a numbness that would not be easily quenched. When you have Daddy issues, you can run to a man to find a carcass to hold you. Outside of my grandmother and my children, most women in my life have not brought me comfort, only disdain. I'm hard pressed not to find jealousy, strife, and gossip. Male or female, I didn't grow up with trust in either sex.

I was trying to solve this murder, not explore my childhood.

Twenty-Four

The Dig

"One does not become enlightened by imagining figures of light, but by making the darkness visible"
—Carl Jung

I felt that if the police were done and did not have funding to excavate, I would need to try myself to uncover the body. And try I did. I contacted Detective Zapata in April of 2011.

Subject: 1968 Murder -- Plans to Dig

Detective Zapata, good morning.

My mother, and some other members of the family, want to begin to dig for the murdered person's remains. While I believe this woman to be Madeline Babcock, we cannot determine identity without a body. As I shared with you, I told my father I would bury her properly and he said, "I know you will." I feel I must finish this. For my family and for her, and her family.

It seems logical to me that we should know something about the process of exhuming a body correctly. There is no other way at this point to find resolution for our family and the dead woman's family, but to try to find her body. It must happen. Of course, Craig (the other person in the room,

who, by the way, held her arms as her throat was slit) is still alive, but I
believe we will find little, if any, help there. Chris Peterson's interview with
Craig determined that Mr. Holbrock would be willing to submit to a lie
detector test, but he said he would NOT be willing to meet with me. If I had
my way, I'd make him meet with me. It seems he just told us what his weak
link is. Confrontation with me. He knows he could ace a lie detector test but
obviously fears my position as a witness. Anyway, I can only have control
over so much.

I told Chris Peterson to stop work. I don't have any more money for this.
If you have any material or know of someone who I could speak with
about the correct procedure to dig for and find her, please let me know. I've
tried my best to keep you in the loop with this-- and that's my intention
with this email.

Thank you, sir.
Jodie

His response to me the following day:

I have an idea, but I'm in training until next week. I'm not sure that I
have a phone number for you still. Would you forward me your number?
I'll call you when I come back next Tuesday.

Foolishly, I got together a posse of my children and other close
friends, enlisted as many shovels as we could find, and went to the
gravesite on my parents' property. I had received permission from my
mother to go ahead and try to dig – try being the operative word here.
Early one morning we all gathered, packed up a dozen shovels (or
more), and started our long drive up to Livingston Mountain. Our first
stop was at my mother's house to tell her we would be down at the
dumpsite beginning the excavation.

Like a queen bee having her hive disturbed my mom wasn't at ease
with her conditional response that we could be there but that was not

going to detour my set determination for the day. We started our walk, just as Dad and Craig had done forty years earlier, through the field down to the sink hole.

The day was brisk and overcast, the cold sank into our bones as we got closer. We gathered ourselves around the dump site. The dump site was now obviously overgrown with briers and littered with various vegetation. This wasn't going to be easy. We started digging. It seems silly looking back, but bones are fragile and could be easily missed with heavy equipment shovels, so we started gently. It also was going to cost money to hire an excavator, and quite honestly, I was scared to come in with such a bang! I knew Mom didn't really want me to dig, so if I was quiet and went about this, she might not stop it.

It didn't take long to discovery that man-powered tools would get us nowhere – fast. I also realized how far we needed to dig to be anywhere close to the body. I needed to hire an excavator with a backhoe. Now that we had placated my mother and she was in the house, I decided to take the step we needed.

It was an extremely cold, damp day in the northwest. My youngest daughter, her ex-husband and their first son went up to my mother's house to get warm. While they were there waiting, my grandson – who was about two -- asked his father who the man was standing in the back room. The room he pointed to was the place where my father spent most of his time.

My ex-son-in-law investigated the room. He saw no one and said, "No one's there, sweetheart."

His son answered emphatically, "Dad, he's right there. The guy in black."

It freaked my ex-son-in-law and daughter out so bad, they left my parents' home and bolted down the mountain, back to town. Evil obviously didn't like us all there that day.

I called local excavator companies and found someone who would come that day. He arrived with his backhoe and we gathered around the site.

After a few minutes, he looked intently at me and said, "Are we digging for a body? I'll still run my backhoe, but I just want to know."

I was taken aback. I had thought about the possibility of this question being posed and had come up with a ridiculous scenario we could tell him about digging for treasure, but when he asked me face to face, I did what was now natural for me to do --I told him the truth. He proceeded.

Mom told us that she remembered that one of the first things my father threw into this sink-hole-dumpsite was an old chest freezer. I told the excavator that we were looking for this old freezer and if we found it, we'd have him stop. Detective Zapata had told me that if we found any evidence of a body, he would employ a cohort professor and his students to aid in the final dig of the dumpsite.

Karen's ex-husband, Tom, came up to see what was going on. He had a conversation with one member of our posse, Joe. He asked if he knew what a sink hole looked like. Joe told him he did not. He took Joe on a small walk to show him how vast a sink hole could be and told him that we may be trying to accomplish the impossible.

The excavator continued to dig. Each shovel of dirt we went through with rakes, trying not to miss anything. The backhoe screeched as it dug through the decades of cans.

The color of the cans indicated an era gone by. As we got closer to the '70s, there were beer and Pepsi cans that we hadn't seen for years but recognized immediately. We were getting closer to the debris of the '60s. We'd been in the dig for hours by now and had come up against a wall. The wall of my sister's driveway.

Tom, my brother-in-law, had told us earlier that day that the main dumpsite was directly underneath the driveway that my sister had built to her house. Was this coincidental that she and my father designed a driveway directly over the dump site? Probably not. But to continue the dig that day, it would mean the demise of her driveway. I didn't have the resources to rebuild the road. We had just gotten to the oldest cans of the day. It was dusk and we had to stop. My heart and soul collapsed into the watery depths of that bottomless sink hole.

I had to tell the excavator to stop. He packed up and drove away with every dream that I had to find that woman. It was over. I remember the strong desire to throw my body on the ground so that there would be nothing between me and the dead lady but my heart and the earth that covered her. I wanted to find her, be close to her again, and tell her I was sorry. I was sorry for her violent, cruel ending. I was sorry that she'd never see her children again. That I was sorry I couldn't bring her back to life and fix this horrible mess.

I came home absolutely devastated. This was my only chance at unearthing and telling her I was filled with misery at the loss of her life. That her haunting dreams had stayed with me all my life. She wasn't forgotten if I kept her alive through my memory, and by telling her story.

When I walked back in my house that day it was filled with those who went to help with the dig. It felt like complete chaos as my mind raced to find closure. There were children running around, and noise – laughter and dinner preparation plans were being discussed. I couldn't engage.

I wanted to die.

I wanted to scream.

I needed to tell her goodbye.

Twenty-Five

Another Voice in the Storm

"It is a joy to be hidden and a disaster not to be found."
-D.W. Winnicott

Healing happens in the most obtrusive ways. You never know when to expect it. It's like a thief in the night, something you can't anticipate the arrival of.

I was preparing for a nice steamy hot Epson salt bath. The bubbles I'd poured in now cascaded above the tempered water. I strategically placed my bath pillow just right so I could ease down into a blissful evening of relaxation. Before I stepped in, I placed my glass of wine, a large glass of ice water, iPhone (of course), and my glasses beside me. I was ready for some down time to myself. I lifted my phone and found my favorite game while detoxing in this humid heaven. I texted my friend to tell her that the bath pillows we'd ordered together were just perfect and I was using mine – I nudged her to use hers as well.

I started playing my game and my right hand was cramping up a bit. It did that often, but this was a very different feeling. It started getting heavier and heavier. Soon, it was so heavy that I had to give in to the feeling. I put my phone in my other hand and dropped my hand into the water. Bingo.

My bathroom had now become the bathroom in the old motel room in '68. My mind's eye flew open. The window of the memory had started with that body memory. I didn't realize what my hand was telling me until I was instantly back in the motel room. Plain as day, I was there, again. I could see all of us there. Dad, Craig, me, but the woman had already been murdered and was missing. The room was full of chaos, and they were moving about quickly, but not orderly. Dad handed me his knife. It was heavy – that was the heaviness that was in my hand. The odd thing about working through tragic memories is the way they come back makes sense when you educate yourself. The body keeps score and the heaviness in my hand led me back.

With the knife in my hand (which makes no difference anymore, except to explain the weight in my hand), Dad told me to follow him into the bathroom. I didn't want to go because they had placed that lady in there. I opened my eyes or were they shut? I wanted to pull myself out of that bathroom and to stop watching in my mind's theater. But now, I was urged back, so I continued. Craig was in the bathroom and the lady was in the bathtub.

The water was running over her neck, and they had her head laid back, sort of cocked in a weird position. It was laid back so far it was like a fish head that had not been cut off all the way and flopped back. Her head just should not in that position.

"It shouldn't look like that," I literally said out loud.

My mind raced as I was watching it again. I started crying rather loudly and intently. The scene played out with the water running over and over her neck. It ran until the blood seemed to be washed away.

By this time, my husband heard me gasping with struggle from the other room and had walked into the bathroom to ask me what was wrong. I told him that I was okay, that I was just seeing something. I tried to catch myself, wind it up, and be done but just continued to blubber quite loudly. I wanted him to just to go away and leave me alone.

The troubled lines on his forehead outlined his fear and concern, "Jodie, you are not okay."

The persuasion on his face got me to get out of the bath. I didn't want to get out of my bath. I just took twenty minutes getting the damn thing set up so I could be peaceful. And then this happened!

I went into the back room with my husband and continued trying to process and get through the memory. It's an extremely unpleasant thing to do. My husband, of course, wanted to just get me back to a better place. But as we watched TV it became clear to him that you don't just wrap one of these flashbacks up in the newspaper like an old dead fish carcass and toss it out. It isn't that easy. I got through the night, had another couple of glasses of wine to still my mind and nerves, and then went into a fitful night's sleep.

About 4:30 AM, I was woken to deep trembling and severe body aches. I saw myself lying in bed the night after the murder in the house on Delaware Lane. The light from the moon was coming through the window and I couldn't stop shaking. I shook so bad that it felt like my head was going to wobble right off my shoulders. My body had shaken in fear and pain before, but this crazy head shake wasn't something I was used to. Now, I was scared again because I didn't know how to stop it. It felt as if my head wanted to wobble right off!

Maybe it was my way as a child to piece together all I had seen. A person's head would not stay in one place severed like that. It would wobble.

I reminded myself that no one would come that night or any night of my childhood to comfort me, but I could now change that.

I remembered being so thirsty.

I just wanted to take a hot bath because I hurt everywhere.

So, you know how you take care of a memory like this? You get up and do the things for that little you that you wanted someone so desperately to do for you then.

I got up at 4:30 am. I got a tall glass of ice water and ran another hot bubble bath. This bubble bath was very much unlike the one I had prepared for myself a few hours before. This bubble bath was to commiserate with and comfort that old friend – the deep tattered part of me who so desperately needed it in 1968. I stayed until the water was cold. I let the water out and filled it up again and drifted into a sleep, right there in that hot water.

That morning, I walked upstairs and climbed into my bed, happy that I'd given myself the gifts I'd wanted before.

I emailed work and let them know that I wouldn't be in for the day. I'd been through this a time or two before and would be worthless at work.

I woke up a few hours later to a tremendous headache. My body ached everywhere, and my soul hurt. I went through the day and wasn't sure how I was going to put this away so that it didn't tear up my life for weeks or even days. I watched movies to try to escape into someone else's story. I went for a nice walk and bought Thai food. I came home and as the night hours would be coming on soon, I needed a plan.

What would my night look like? Would I see them washing out her neck over and over as I tried to go to sleep? Would I go to sleep and wake up with another nightmare of something else that I hadn't remembered and be terrified all over again? I couldn't know for sure what was going to happen, but I was getting better at trying.

I decided not to have anything to drink as the night fell in, because I'd need all my strength to get through this and I wanted to figure it out.

A few hours before I got into bed, I got a severe bout of diarrhea. This carried on for about the first hour I was in bed. My body was tremendously trepidatious going into the dark hours of night. As I lay there crying out to God, He answered me.

I watched as Jesus walked into that motel room and picked me up. He put me in his arms and held me tight. He walked over to the bathroom door, and He closed it. I heard Him tell me that I didn't have to go in there anymore. I didn't have to continue to watch. He'd stopped it for me. Now, I was equipped with an answer. Every time my mind wanted to go back and replay that scene (which would be a vicious cycle), I'd only go back to the door and see it closed and my mind could stop.

The vicious cycling was over.

And then I asked Him if He could go into that room where I had been laying that night in '68, on Delaware Lane. The aloneness that encroached on me and the absolute pain inside and out that night needed to be quieted with comfort. I asked if He would lie down beside me on that bed and just hold me. I asked Him to make the shaking stop. I asked Him to help me be warm and feel loved.

I felt the peace as I watched Him comply with every request. I fell into a peaceful sleep that night. I woke up in the morning and was ready to get on with life. It was now just a memory, not active but still. His presence and voice had calmed that storm.

Twenty-Six

The Witness, The Accomplice

"Generations do not cease to be born, and we are responsible to them because we are the only witness they have."
—James Baldwin

I cannot bring the dead woman back, but I am a witness to her last moments on earth. I fought hard for her, for her family, and for me. The local police opened a case and did what they could to help. They told me they would need a body or a confession. Period.

A confession.

That gave me a reason to try.

I went to see Craig one last time to record his confession. Why not? I'd tried everything and everyone else. He was the last hope remaining.

The trip my parents took with Craig in 1964, historically saved by them all in the picture of the three of them at *Stardust*, was also recorded by my dad. I was given two CDs by my mother and one of them held that road trip. This was my ticket in to bring to Craig.

I called him and confirmed he'd be home. I told him I had footage of their trip together and wanted to share it with him. He was eager for my visit.

I was not.

My husband, Jeff, and I arrived at his house at midday. I brought my computer to be sure we could play the CDs in the hope that this would be disarming and lend a friendship quality to this inquisition.

Before we walked in, we both started the recorders on our phones.

The video began and Craig's disposition changed. He was delighted to see my parents.

"There she is!" His face lit up with a healthy grin and his hand ran smoothly along the countertop as he watched my mother.

"We were your family back then, weren't we," I asked.

"Oh, yes – yes, you were," his gaze never left the video. "I loved Crissy."

Our visit lasted well over an hour. Here are excerpts of the recording. His words speak the loudest, so there's no need to change them.

Recording Transcript:

> *Jodie: We didn't do it. I remember you crying that day saying, "Stan, why'd you do it."*
>
> *Craig: Crying?*
>
> . . .
>
> *Jodie: When he was dying . . .*
>
> *Craig: Yeah?*
>
> *Jodie: He and I were talking about this and I said, "Dad, I have felt horrible since that moment" and he said, "I'm sorry. I'm so sorry." I told him -- that I would fix it. I don't know how. I need your help.*
>
> *Craig: No, forget it, forget it. I don't even recognize who it is, period. Jodie: I don't know I was too little, but I remember she had blonde hair and she was little and the only picture I could find I thought -- it might be her.*
>
> *Craig: I don't know.*

Craig: I don't know, I wouldn't -- I wouldn't worry about it myself. I'd just forget about it.

Jodie: How do you? Be peaceful with it? Dad wasn't always peaceful with it.

Craig: Well, that's his problem.

Jodie: And you were fine with it. I wasn't. It was hard for me.

Craig: Well, hang in there another thirty or forty years and you'll get over it.

(laughing)

Jodie: Well, there you go.

Craig: See, I just solved your problem.

Jodie: Another thirty or forty years to get over it.

Craig: Yeah.

Next excerpt at 00:07:45

Jodie: Maybe if I knew this was her, I could do a memorial or something 'cause I'm not gonna go there and dig and maybe I can't.

Jodie: I hired this guy, and we took it all the way down and we would have to take that Rd out so I'm not going to do that. And it's all over, it's over like that's gone.

Craig: Just forget the whole dang thing.

Craig: I think that's your best move.

Jodie: Is it?

Craig: I really do. What does he think (motioning to Jeff)

Jodie: Probably he wants me to, too.

Jodie: I just wanna help -- crazy.

Craig: No, don't worry about it.

Jeff: Well, I think the most important thing is if it could be figured out is for her family

Craig: Yeah

Jeff: More so than anybody else on this side

Craig: Yeah

Jodie: I know, but I can't know who. She is for sure, right? I just can't.

Craig: Nope -- you think I'd remember who she was. She'd look familiar.

Jodie: I know, but I remember her hair falling down on her shoulders, right?

Craig: Let's forget it.

Craig: She does not look familiar at all.

Jodie: So maybe that's not her.

Craig: Could be! Yeah.

Jodie: I don't know. I just remember that she was small. She was kind.

Craig: What was her name?

Jodie: I think it was Lynn, wasn't it? Our Madeline. I don't know.

Jodie: So, you don't remember.

Craig: I don't know.

Jodie: I don't remember her name either.

Jeff: Her middle name is Anna.

Craig: Anna, Anna, Madeline – nope, Madeline Anna Babcock, I don't remember that at all.

Craig: Nope.

Craig: Nope. Nope. Nope. So, if I were you, I would just forget the whole thing. I really would. It isn't necessary to you to take your time, energy, Intelligence to do anything. You don't really need to.

Jodie: Well then why'd Dad say, "I know you will?"

Craig: Oh, who knows?

Jodie: 'cause he was feeling bad about it? He said, "I'm sorry, I'm so sorry."

Craig: Nope. Nope, just let it go.

Jodie: It's hard.

Craig: Yeah.

Jodie: And you always want to. I just want to do the, you know – what's right by him. But he was the one that did it.

Craig: He'll forgive you. He's probably watching you right now -- looking down or looking up.

Jodie: No, we can't. . .

Craig: I don't know where he went.

Jodie: Exactly, he could be, right?

Jodie: That's right, that's very true.

Craig: Right now, the other.

Jodie: Just let it go on.

Craig: Yeah -- I would.

That was the end of our conversation.
Would you "just let it go?"

Twenty-Seven

A Prisoner of Hope

"You remember too much, my mother said to me recently.
Why hold onto all that? And I said,
Where can I put it down?"

—*The Glass Essay* by Anne Carson

Police closed the case. In Vancouver Police Report V08-17083, the assigned detective's closing statements convicted me as an abused little girl that made shit up and couldn't be believed. Basically, in his closing words he exonerated both of my parents. He writes:

In January 2012, I examined a medical record Jodie provided to prove the accuracy and reliability of her memory. Unfortunately, the record supports neither. According to Jodie's memory it was "night time" June 8, 1968 and "dark outside". Her Dad and Craig are outside the car at the bottom of the hill burying the murder victim. She remembers they headed home after that and once home her Dad has a medical emergency which causes him to go to the hospital. The medical record dates her Dad's hospitalization at 12:55am, June, 9, 1968. It reads in part "wife states patient is a diabetic...went to sleep about seven pm (June 8)... has been unable to be aroused since..." A weather almanac shows that on June 8, 1968 sunset was at 8:56pm. Considering this and the hospital record it would've been impossible for Stan Steele to be outside in the dark with Craig Holbrook during the night of June 8, 1968, burying a murder victim with Jodie White nearby. I've reviewed this case with a sincere desire to assist Jodie White in her pursuit for justice for a woman she believed was murdered in Vancouver, WA. However, I can't ignore the facts which oppose the validity of her statements. These facts weaken Jodie's credibility and bring into question the rationality behind continued investigation. Without a clear base of facts, I can no longer pursue this matter. I'm therefore concluding this investigation and closing it without further review.

This detective interviewed my mom, Karen, and Craig but it is my understanding that my father was never interviewed. Why? I hold my mother to a deep accountability for this cover up.

She knew then. She knows now.

Just as the detective told Pat, my mother had lied in 1968 to cover up the truth and she lied again for the very same reason. Here's the email from Pat dated 11/16/2013:

I forgot to tell you Det. Zapata said your Mother told him your dad was home all day on June 8th 1968 and your mother was worried about your dad not feeling well that day and made him lie down because he was not feeling well .And she took him to the hospital that night about 7 P.M. Jodie do you have the actual record of your Dad's stay at the Hospital could you send me a copy . I believe in you but when I write to the FBI they will ask me how is it I know when Madeline was murdered I need to have a copy of your Dads admission to that Hospital . I hope you can send me a copy. We will prevail in this. Look at the hard time the Venice police gave to my mom and I just tried to file a report and they still refused to do so. The truth is on our side no matter.

The hospital record admitting my dad states that the patient "went to sleep about 7 pm and could not be aroused since, even when immersed into a cold bath." They indicate he was foamy at the mouth and appeared somewhat rigid.

I saw my father in many reactions, some severe enough to call 911. None as severe as a foamy mouth and rigid. It would take many hours to sink to this level.

What really happened was the three of us hadn't eaten all day. I saw dad drinking beer up at the property. When dad woke me up in the car that night, it was clear by his bizarre low-insulin-induced behavior that he was well into a reaction. He passed out in my lap almost immediately. Our house was at least twenty-five to thirty minutes into town. When Craig carried him into the house, he was already unconscious, and he laid him on the sofa. Mom freaked out and called his parents and they called his brother. They immediately came over and put him into an ice bath. My uncle's letter confirms that. Then, when he did not respond they took him to the hospital.

My mother knew exactly what she was doing that night by lying to the hospital about what happened and creating a different timeline. Why didn't she tell them what she told me, that she knew we had been working at the property? You give an alibi when you know there is a reason for one. My mother put on record the very thing that would exonerate him fifty years later.

She wants us to believe that her diabetic husband went to sleep on the couch at 7 pm and lay there until he had to be thrown into an ice bath and eventually admitted to the hospital at 12:55 am. He lay there for five and a half hours growing rigid and she did nothing until he frothed at the mouth? No way!

This kind of reaction does not happen in a few hours. It just wouldn't have happened like that. I watched my father go in and out of diabetic reactions my entire life and so did she.

Relocating to another state, I tried one last time to find help. On Sunday, March 21, 2021, at 9:02 am, I send this email to the Head Prosecutor for the Major Crimes Unit at the Clark County Prosecutor's office. My subject line is "Request for Search Warrant to Exhume Human Remains."

> *Dear Ms. Klein,*
>
> *I give you this statement, under the penalty of perjury, under the laws of the state of Washington, that the statement I am bringing you below is true and correct.*
>
> *This is a request you most likely don't receive every day. When I was three years old (2 months shy of turning four), I witnessed my father, James S. Steele and a family friend, Donald Craig Holbrook, rape and murder a woman in a room at the Riverside Motel on Highway 14. They then drove the body to his 40 acres at 6121 NE Lessard Road, Camas, Washington, and buried her in a sinkhole. The date of the murder was June 8, 1968.*
>
> *My only request to your office is to ask the court to issue me a search warrant to go exhume the human remains of the murdered victim.*
>
> *To date, I have tried to take the appropriate course of action by:*
>
> *In 2006, I went to Vancouver City Police and gave them my statement. They found me credible and opened a case (VPD Case No. 08017083). When my father passed away, the case was closed for a minor discrepancy they*

believed they found (most likely just a reason to close a very old case). My mother made a statement on the hospital records in 1968 that my father went to sleep on the couch at 7 pm and couldn't be woken up, so they took him to the hospital. I will refer you to the recorded statements I've made in videos explaining this in detail (link below). Detective Zapata closes the case with, "if he was sleeping on the couch, he couldn't have been at the property working late at night burying the body." My mother lied for him then, and she still covers for him today.

After my father's death, the detectives interviewed me wherein I told them that my father apologized to me two separate times for the murder when I said I had lived with guilt for leaving the room alive, when she did not. At that, the detectives told me that it sounded like a true confession to them. Sgt. Creager said, "You can ask Zapata, but that is how these men are - they confess to the smallest thing they can." In that conversation with my father (he died the next morning) I told him I would bring the woman's body up and have her returned to her family and buried properly. My father said, "I know you will." I need to make this right.

After all was said and done, the detectives told me they needed a confession or a body to proceed with an investigation.

My attempt at gaining a confession from Donald Holbrook: I have gone to Donald Holbrook's home (I have the recording of that conversation) and although he does not deny having been an accomplice to this murder, he will not concede to help.

Exhuming the Human Remains: The murder victim is still buried on my mother's property at 6121 NE Lessard Road, Camas, WA. I attempted an excavation once but was forced to stop because my sister and father built a gravel road leading to her home over the deepest part of the dump, essentially blocking the area where the body would most likely be. In 1968, my father turned this burial plot into the family dump and filled it with rubbish for over 20 years. Today, I have the resources I did not have then *to pay for an appropriate excavation. I believe this time we should start our approach behind the dump, which could leave her road intact.*

This is where your office can hopefully help me. I am not asking you to do anything other than ask the court to grant me access to the property so I can bring in an experienced excavator and unearth the human remains that were buried there in 1968 by James Steele and Craig Holbrook.

I will do this at my full expense.

I understand the police department and county do not have the means to help in such cold cases. If I am unable to find the body, I will put the property back in the same state it is in today, but I fully believe we will find her. My mother told me one of the first things my father threw into the dump was an old chest freezer - if I find the chest freezer, the body will be close. The property is located on a rural, undeveloped piece of land, which for a short while longer, is still in the possession of my mother.

My mother is preparing to sell the land. I had a niece call me to let me know that the sell is imminent. Before it is handed off to someone who may develop this land, I need to excavate and return this murdered woman to her rightful place - with her family (I have a video explaining why I believe the missing person Madeline Anna Babcock is this murdered woman). I do not want to trespass or break any laws and my mother is not in favor of another excavation as she believes it will devalue her land.

A search warrant may be issued by the court upon your request. I need that to bring in an experienced excavator and unearth the human remains that are buried at 4444 NE River Road, Camas, Washington.

Lastly, I threw this out to the Reddit community to find help. This was where I learned I could go directly to you for help. They also told me to create videos of my case and what facts I have found through the PI I hired and the Vancouver Police Department. You can find those videos here: YouTube @amissingpersonsstory-madel2815.

The reply:

From: Cnty PA General Delivery Prosecutor@clark.wa.gov>

Sent: Monday, April 12, 2021, 11:03 AM

To: Jodie Tedder

Subject: Request for Search Warrant to Exhume Human Remains

Hi Jodie –

Thank you for reaching out. You will want to forward this information over to the Vancouver Police Department for them to follow up on.

A final plea to the Vancouver Police Department on April 13, 2021:

Dear Chief of Police,

With one final plea, I am requesting your help. Sir, this plea is not just for my own healing and completion. This request is for the voice of a woman murdered in 1968.

Your department opened a case (VPD Case No. 08017083) and then closed it. Detective Zapata was respectful and did his job with a case that is racked and riddled with limitations. The limitation that I was only two months away from being four when I witnessed the murder. My father apologized on his death bed, the accomplice told me to just let it go, but I cannot. The case was closed due to a "discrepancy". My mother lied in 1968 that my father went to sleep on the couch at 7 pm there could not have been burying a body on the property late at night as I said. She still lies to cover to this today. The accomplice, Craig Holbrook is still alive. Justice should be served.

When Zapata closed the case, I was told they'd need a confession or a body. Today, I have the means to hire an experienced excavator and un-earth her remains. I also have the stability to stand through this task. If my memory is in question, please call Dr. Foster Reams. He has a master's in child psychology and has worked with me for over 15 years. His number is 555.555.555. He can explain traumatic memories, how they return and why I am credible. My mother has never been counseled and is not credible in her truth telling of anything about our past.

This murder did happen.

I only need a search warrant to go excavate. I want to do this with
law enforcement so there can be peace around the effort. I wrote to the
Prosecutor's office, and they told me to go back to the VPD.

Here I am. Making one final plea for help. See more details below in my
email to the prosecutor.

The burden for closure relentless.

I met with my mother one last time to ask for her help. I told
her that I had an excavator service hired and ready to proceed, hoping
that if this line of help failed, I could receive assistance again from the
Vancouver Police Department.

The Chief of Police surprisingly called and said he had assigned a
new detective to look over the case.

Karen and Mom called me and Jeff to tell us access to the property
was denied. I foolishly pleaded for her to remember any love she might
have had for me. Tim said, "Your sister has planted trees there now."
Mom deeded more land to Karen and the dump was now on her property, not my mother's. Explaining that I had asked for a search warrant,
I told them that the VPD was looking at the case again.

The next day I received a call from the new detective. Karen called
and connived. In flowery deceit she explained that she allowed me
access once and was just not willing to allow access for an excavation
again. Heartbroken, I felt betrayed but then again didn't have higher
expectations of my family.

I replied with this email to the detective, Karen, my mother, and the
grandchildren of the missing woman who found my YouTube channel
and just reached out to me:

Dear All,

For the record, Karen DID NOT allow the first dig. That is a complete
lie. She stated on the phone how she was not notified the first time and how
wrong it was. My husband heard the entire conversation. Now I'm told that

she tells you she allowed it, and it was very kind of her? That is an absolute lie. And, yet I am the liar here.

It's baffling quite honestly. Karen and Jezebel Steele obstruct justice by telling their story three different ways and that's ok? No one checks their character to determine why they lie? These women spend their life changing our family's reality and their own reality, and they are believed? Baffling. It's a small reach within the family to learn who these wretched women are to most family members, but you detectives talk with only them.

I am including the missing person's grandchildren. They deserve to be part of this now, too.

Lynn's grandchildren, I received a call from Detective Ripp this morning. I appreciate his time. He told me there is not enough evidence to proceed with a search warrant. He said that the matching dates in June 1968 (the 8th and the 11th) are too far apart to match albeit your Aunt Pat and her mother didn't even make that police report for some months. The recall of this missing woman showing me her purse and the email where her sister confirms that this was a "signature move" of this missing woman. None of those matches qualify anything to the Vancouver Police Department as anything of significance.

I am going to the media, and I am consulting an attorney. This is not over. This murdered woman deserves a proper burial. I will do all I can to allow that to happen.

Karen - your father wanted this, too. I am sorry to have even asked you and Mom to help. What a shameful life you all live. You can hide your own truth all you want. I will not allow you to hide the truth for this woman.

I just wanted to give you all notice.

This is not over.

My youngest daughter had driven through the night to be with us for the potential excavation. When they arrived, we had to tell them it wasn't happening. We all took my mother to breakfast that morning. Two started their phones to record the conversation.

When asked if she believed my father murdered this woman, without hesitation she told us, "Yes, I'm sure he did it and I'm sure it's Madeline. I was there when these memories were returning to Jodie. She told me the woman was a small, blonde woman. And then I read through the documentation and had worked with the judge she mentioned here in Washington. That placed her in the state of Washington."

"Mom, why did you say Dad went to sleep at 7 o'clock that night? He was twenty-nine years old and never took naps," I asked.

"No – I don't know. He was dead drunk. Craig was carrying him. I was so angry."

She went on, "There wouldn't be record of them checking into the motel room because your grandmother cleaned there. But I'm sure he did it. He couldn't sleep during that time. He was off and I knew there was something wrong."

The conversation turned to the lie detector test that Cinnamon had my father complete – he passed it. Mom said, "Oh yeah, he told me later that if you take enough drugs, anyone can pass that test."

Do you think she told the investigating officer that little fact that Dad shared with her?

She muttered under her breath to me, "I think there are more bodies on the property."

"Why do you always say that?"

Her answer held no facts. "I just wouldn't put it past him. He was a psychopath. I'm getting off that property."

Did she know more? Did she share that belief with the investigating officers?

She sold her land. The dumpsite where the murdered woman's body still lies was given to my sister through a boundary-line adjustment. What a gift.

I wish I could bring more than that date and my witness to the table, but I cannot. I have tried. I wish I could fill pages with proof, but many crimes come without proof. The crimes of the worst degree often have no evidence.

Liars are far better at telling their stories than their victims are at telling the truth.

The woman's body has not been exhumed and returned to her family.

Conclusion

"I have no greater joy than to hear that my children will walk in truth."
3 John 1:4

I'm not mad at the cops. They did what they could. While my story is an extreme example of searching for justice, it is very ordinary when it comes to making a case against an abuser. They seem to always win. I know it's a stretch to use the word always, but in a comparative sense it seems fitting. The number of abusers who walk away uncharged is staggering. Abusers begin their stories with each victim built around lies. Their lies continue as their abuse and grooming grows. Lying is just second nature to them so they are unaffected when approached by the truth or a lie detector test.

Victims come from a very different experience. Even before the abuse emerges, abusers attempt to blur boundaries of what is appropriate, inappropriate, normal, or abnormal. Then, before long, the predator introduces secrecy to gain cooperation, participation, and silence. If you want their love (well – better stated, you need their love) then you will do as they say and never betray those secrets. You break every rule that God built inside of you and are no longer in touch with things as they are. You must deny reality. They are your rule makers, your god. Everything they want from you, you learn to give them.

At three, no one has defenses. Then, they weaken your God-given fortifications as you grow so they can pluck from you what they want. The essence of innocence is stolen. As the waves came from the oceans of deceivers in our youth, our winds must now blow a torrential storm back in the face of abuse. The worst classification of abuse might be the journey against the winds of our abusers calling out accusations against us – we are liars, we struggled with mental illness.

This is not a head issue. These are issues of the heart.

The problem for the victim is that the ghost cars of reality and truth have been wrought with confusion, self-rejection, and self-doubt. It's been my faith, my children, my husband, and the many others around me that have carried me through.

What does matter is that I have used the tools that God gave me to find redemption. The redemption of a little girl who had no voice, no thoughts that could be her own, and a tale that hadn't been told. I could not find recovery from such crimes, but my life could be redeemed.

In passing one day, I told my oldest nephew that I remember watching my mother in the bathtub. She would make me stand at the edge of the tub and just watch her.

My oldest nephew responded with, "Aunt Jodie, I totally remember watching Grandma in the bathtub too. In fact, when I lived with Grandma, she always wanted to take my youngest boy and give him a bath. It creeped me out and I wouldn't let her."

I should have been stunned to hear his memory but had learned through years of sharing that the truth was not only being heard it was sometimes corroborated. I shared this story with my youngest daughter.

Are you going to guess what she said?

Yep! Almost without skipping a beat she said, "Mom, I remember watching Grandma in the bathtub, too. At our big house."

This accounting represents three generations, spanning over thirty years apart, but one thing remained -- an abuser was at the heart of them.

If we don't tell our stories we keep ourselves and others imprisoned by crimes we didn't commit. The reason we tell our stories is for freedom. Not just freedom for ourselves but for everybody whom we love.

For me one had to die for others to remain.

The truth is that I have gone as far as I can go with putting the body of the murdered women to rest. I have not returned her to her family. I still want to fight for her, but I have written her story here. That mattered to her sister, and it mattered greatly to me. Her story will not be forgotten.

Indeed, there is a battle. The longest battle in the world's history. The battle between light and darkness. Good and evil. God and Satan. We must decide what side we're going to fight for. We all fight for a side; it just depends on which side we place our armor. It doesn't matter when we show up to fight. What does matter is what side we choose to fight for.

Truth will outlast any campaigns mounted against it, no matter how strong or vociferous. It is invincible. It's only a matter of which generation is willing to face it and in so doing, protect future generations.

While I was trying to survive, I was often judged by my failures. I didn't let that stop me. Not only did I accept myself, but I have learned how to honor my failures and learn from them. In the deepest part of who I am, I didn't see them as failures. I was in a true battle. The battle of good and evil. Light and dark. The fleshly sins of overeating, smoking, drinking – all of them had little to do with the deepest battle that raged within me.

I conquered life one minute at a time, day by day I grew.

The battle to shed light onto the great darkness I had come from. That's why I didn't judge myself. I was in a fight. I wasn't standing on the roadside watching it go by as a spectator.

The night that I was so drunk I couldn't lift my head up off the floor, and my fireplace glass doors blew out around me. I commemorate that fact today. I gave myself the courage to find the pain. I gave myself the courage to live with the pain, uncomfortable and raw! I celebrate that I had the honor of getting to know myself, owning my deep desire to let my pain free. My drive for freedom was relentless as it flew towards its flight.

It took years to understand the guilt I had for not allowing myself to explore my pain. I held myself in contempt for not allowing my own freedom. I gave it to everyone else. Even though my parents didn't allow me to feel or speak about anything, it was a God-given right and I fought for it. Many won't. I don't hold myself in condemnation for drinking too much that night or any other night. Rather, I understand that night as a small victory – I was walking in the truth. I am not called to be good; I am called to be Godly.

I am in the true battle of life.

The rain from those dark oppressive clouds have ceased now. I have stopped living by the created version of myself that someone else made. Following God has taught me one thing -- He loves me because of all my human frailties. Those weaknesses make my strength.

At my father's funeral, my cousin Stacey walked up to me with a smile and gave me a hug. We were chatting and her father, Uncle Mike, came up, put his hand out to hers, and whisked her away from me. Why? Was I guilty of the murder? Was I guilty of being a liar? Or was I condemned for my voice?

Time and time again I have been rejected or put away by so many. I stand convinced of this: what it takes to survive is a tremendous accomplishment. And accomplishment trumps judgment. If you're busy enough with living your own life and finding your own accomplishments, you don't have time to judge.

With a heart that is sometimes heavy, but not hardened, I carry on. With the rest of my time on this planet, I'm gonna cook, I'm gonna love, I'm gonna sing, and I'm gonna learn.

As an homage to all missing persons and the families searching for them, I'd like to leave this.

On April 16, 2013, in an email I received from Pat, Madeline's sister, she writes,

"We were very close and sang together a lot. I dream a lot more of her now.

I lived in Venice California at the beach apartments on the boardwalk. I knew the trashman. I lived there for twelve years prior. He is the reason I wrote this song."

> *Yea He's Got the Rhythm Trashman Yea He's Got the Rhythm.*
> *Trashman, now he's got a rhythm*
> *Trashman, yea he's got a rhythm*
> *He picks up the can's and swing's them up on the truck*
> *It's all kind of dirt and all kinds of smuck, Trashman*
> *He does a job most people won't do, and probably gets paid much more than you do Trashman*
> *He faces reality every single day that's a heck of a lot more than most of us can say Trashman.*
> *They all went on strike in the city of New York, yet he came right back, and he cleaned the mess all up trashman*
> *Now you gotta give credit where credit is due*
> *Trashman does a job that most of us won't do Trashman*
> *The job isn't great and it sure isn't grand and you gotta admit there'd be a mess in this land without the help of the handy Trashman*
> *He probably knows more of what life's all about because he pick's it all up then throw's it all out Trashman*

Written by Patricia A. Foy on April 4, 1967.

Do coincidences exist? In my research for this book, I ordered a secondhand copy of *My Dark Places* by James Ellroy. The book is about the author's mother, who was murdered when he was a child. I picked the book up, flipped it open and there lay the receipt for its original purchase.

It was originally purchased at a bookstore called *Small World Books* in Venice Beach, California, on April 25, 2013. I lived in the state of Washington at the time and ordered it online through Amazon on June 19, 2020.

The last known address of the missing woman that we believe is the murder victim was – yep, Venice Beach, California.

Is this a coincidence? I do not believe so. God is the witness to all crimes. He is your witness, and He is mine. Never give up!

The best is yet to come. Of this I am truly certain. And I'm going to continue to tell my story. All my stories. I have that right and no person can tell me to stop. I believe that each of us has more than just a right to tell our stories – it is our destiny.

I had the most incredible dream of my grandma El the other night. I come upon her house, which is now lived in by other people, but still owned by family. When

I turn the corner leading up to her street, piles of snow billow over her barely visible lawn. When I come closer to her porch, I can see bunkers made of snow. They are the most exquisitely formed shields I have ever seen. I look up and see the delicateness of each snowflake as if the frozen wind had blown them masterfully into this design. I thanked her in my dream for her discernable protection. And, just as those snowflakes could easily be broken in their delicate way, so was my grandmother-- fragile and small but full of a fierce love. She shielded me in her unique and fragile way from all that she could. I pray that this delicate but strong protection follows you.

I am in love with each new thing I learn. I am cultivating the ability to love myself despite my shortcomings. I am forever grateful to a God who didn't walk away from me when everyone else had.

Thankful beyond measure for this journey that brought me out.

Grateful for the people whom God put in my path who helped me.

Having the courage to write this story is one of the things I am most appreciative for. I have returned to myself. Fully restored. Fully functioning and making my own mistakes now.

There's this beautiful scripture that says: "I have fought the good fight, I have finished the race, and I have kept my faith." Writing those words makes me cry. My tears recognize the battle scars and the warrior's fatigue. My final race only finished when I arrive on the other side and take my place with God and his Angels.

Until then every finish line for me just starts another race.

I remain forever hopeful.

Jodie Tedder is the writer and author of *A Prisoner by No Crime of My Own*. She courageously and authentically shares her trek of triumphing over a hellish childhood through years of intensive therapy. Explore with her as she walks you through her pursuit of justice for the woman she watched be killed. Originally from the Pacific Northwest, Jodie has recently relocated to the big skies of Montana. In her free time, she volunteers for the CASA program, spends time enjoying her love of cooking by hosting dinner parties (where she always finds room to add another seat), and walks her Old English Sheepdog, Jax, on the mountain trails.

Jodie pens daily on her blog about overcoming a tragic childhood. It's story-telling for the brokenhearted.

Keep in touch with Jodie's social media:
Website: https://prisonerbynocrimeofmyown.com/
Twitter: @JTedder11
Instagram: prisonerbynocrimeofmyown
Podcast on Spotify and other platforms: A Prisoner by No Crime of Own
The Vanished Podcast: Madeline Babcock, Episode 335

www.ingramcontent.com/pod-product-compliance
Lightning Source LLC
Chambersburg PA
CBHW022049020426
42335CB00012B/611